The Best Sex of Your Life

The BEST

Sex of your LIFE

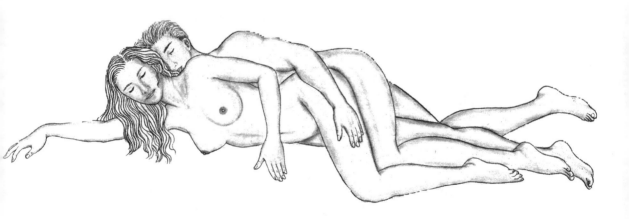

JAMES WHITE Ph.D.

with

PETER KENT

BARRICADE BOOKS | NEW YORK

Published by Barricade Books Inc.
150 Fifth Avenue
New York, NY 10011

Interior design and page layout by CompuDesign

Printed in the United States of America.

Library of Congress Cataloging-in-Publication Data

White, James, Doctor.
    The best sex of your life / James White with Peter Kent.
        p. cm.
    ISBN 1-56980-088-X
    1. Sex instruction. 2. Sex. 3. Sex—Health aspects.
    I. Kent, Peter. II. Title.
    HQ31.W498 1996
    613.9'6—dc20   96-24936
                                            CIP

First Printing

To
Dolores
for the inspiration and love
I've always waited for.
—Jim

We'd like to dedicate this book to all the subjects of our study
(at the University of California, San Diego), who had sex as
often as possible in the unselfish pursuit of scientific knowledge.

Contents

Introduction

Welcome to *The Best Sex of Your Life!* You are about to embark on a course of study designed with one idea in mind . . . that you can radically improve your sex life. There are plenty of books about sex, but this one is different. It's no A to Z of weird and wonderful sexual athletics, it's not an encyclopedia of sexual techniques, or a compendium of sexual know-how. It's a step-by-step guide to put a spark back into your sex life.

In telling you what you must do to improve your sex life, this book digresses a little from the normal fare of sex manuals. In the field of sexual instruction an important area has been neglected—the effect of health and physical fitness on sexual desire, performance, and enjoyment. Most books about sex concentrate solely on the physical act, and forget entirely that desire and physical ability come first. If you don't feel sexy, if you are too out of condition to care about sex, all the sex books in the world won't improve your sex life. As you'll learn, though, physical fitness directly relates to sexual fitness—fit people think about sex more frequently, pursue sexual opportunities more vigorously, and make love more often. They also have more orgasms than people who are out of condition. So we've started this book with a look at how exercise, diet, and drugs affect your sexual enjoyment, and what you can do about it.

We have also covered another area that many sex books forget—knowledge about your desires and those of your partner. We'll help you and your partner discover what sexual techniques you each enjoy, and get more in sync with each other's desires. With these basic issues covered—physical fitness and sexual compatibility—you'll be ready for the best sex of your life.

Most of the modules in this book are focused on specific sexual techniques, from fellatio and cunnilingus to finding the G spot and breast stimulation. Work through them from beginning to end, or each evening just pick one that looks fun. Whether it's toys and games, extended arousal, or copycat lovers, you'll find your sexual exploration will enliven your lovemaking tremendously, pulling you out of old ruts and onto new roads to pleasure.

Module 1

Sexual Exercise— Kegels and Testicular Raises

In the Introduction we discussed how exercise can improve your sex life. We'll start with exercise that has a direct effect on sexual function. You can exercise and strengthen your sexual muscles, and in doing so improve your sex life. We're talking about *Kegel* (pronounced "kay-gel") exercises, named after gynecologist Dr. A. H. Kegel, who first promoted their use. They are used to exercise the *pubococcygeal* muscles—which you'll often hear referred to as the PC muscles. You've probably heard of women doing these exercises, though you may not be aware that men can do them, too.

It has long been known that Kegels could benefit women, and, in turn, their partners. Exercising these muscles has been prescribed for women for thousands of years as a way to develop their sexual abilities. Female slaves with good PC muscle control were often sold for very high prices, and a number of ancient sexual texts refer to the ability of the woman to grasp the penis tightly with her vagina. (The *Kama Sutra* says, "When the woman forcibly holds in her yoni [vagina] the lingam [penis] after it is in, it is called the 'mare's position.' This is learned by practice only, and is chiefly found among the women of the Andra country." Lucky men of Andra!)

Research shows that the benefits of Kegels to a woman are quite clear:

- Strengthening the vaginal muscles can help the woman achieve more powerful orgasms.

- Kegels may improve clitoral sensation and perhaps even help the woman achieve multiple orgasms.

- They help tighten the vagina, making intercourse more pleasurable for the man.

- In particular, they improve vaginal tightness and tone after childbirth.

- A woman with really good control can direct the penis to the most sensitive area of the vagina during intercourse, especially in the woman-on-top positions.

- A few very lucky women with excellent PC-muscle control can bring themselves to orgasm simply by squeezing the muscles repeatedly. (That must keep them happy at work!)

- Good control provides a wonderful way to please the male partner; the woman can squeeze and massage the penis with her vagina. She can "milk" the penis, rhythmically contracting it around the penis as he comes inside her.

In his book, *Male Sexuality*, Bernie Zilbergeld suggests that Kegel exercises—or testicular raises—may help men improve their sex lives, too. These claims are unsubstantiated in the medical literature, but that's not necessarily because they are not true . . . simply that this hasn't been studied to a great degree. Male "Kegels" may, indeed, have beneficial results. Contracting the muscles in the pelvic area near the base of the penis makes them stronger and increases circulation of blood in the pelvic area. Some therapists and researchers claim that these exercises also help a man develop better control of orgasm, and make it more pleasurable. Certainly they give a degree of penile control, the ability to move the penis and to make it throb. A woman may enjoy the new erotic sensations of having her partner's penis pulsing inside her vagina during intercourse, in the same way that it's exciting for him to have her vagina "grab" his penis. And the man will enjoy the sensation, too. It'll make the vagina feel tighter, and his penis will feel almost "alive" as he churns inside his partner.

So let's see how these Kegel exercises work, for both the man and the woman.

✻ ✻ The Female Kegels ✻ ✻

Try to find your PC muscles the next time you go to the bathroom. While urinating, clamp down with the muscles "down there," and see if you can stop the flow of urine. (Or simply imagine yourself urinating, and use the muscles you'd have to employ to stop urinating in midstream.) You are using the PC muscles to do this.

Now that you know where the muscles are, try contracting them. With your legs open just a little, contract the muscles for two or three seconds, then relax them. Repeat ten times. If you want to be quite sure that you are working the correct muscles, lie on a bed and insert a finger into your vagina. When you contract the PC muscles, you'll feel the vagina grasp and tug on your finger.

Do these exercises four or five times a day. You'll soon feel the muscle contractions becoming tighter and more defined. Try to link the exercises to some activity, so you don't forget to do them. Each time you go to the bathroom, for instance, finish up by doing your Kegels. Each time you stop at a traffic light, or have a cup of coffee, do your Kegels. You can do them quite discreetly—nobody has to notice!

There are a couple of other Kegel exercises. There's the *flutter.* You contract the muscles very quickly, so they pulse. You are not holding the contraction, you are contracting, relaxing, contracting rapidly. Do about ten of these flutters, pause, then do ten more. Do about five or six "sets" of these exercises, several times a day. As your muscles strengthen you can increase the number of flutters.

Another exercise is the *elevator:* you are trying to "pull" the opening of your vagina up to the top of your vagina. That's how it feels, anyway. Pull up, but stop a couple of times on the way up. When you get to the top of the elevator, hold the contraction tightly, then release, allowing the elevator to go back down to the ground floor. Try two or three of these, a couple of times a day.

By the way, if you want some help in exercising your PC muscles, you can buy a special Kegel tool that is inserted into the vagina and which you must grasp. You can buy these through some sex shops and through catalogs such as the Xandria Collection (800-242-2823).

✿ ✿ Using Your New-Found Strength ✿ ✿

Believe me, ladies, your partner will appreciate your new-found strength. Men love the sensation of thrusting into a tight vagina. You can now play a number of games with your vagina and his penis. You can squeeze tightly as he thrusts into you, increasing the friction on his penis and pulling the skin of the penis down the shaft. Or you can detain him as he moves out, squeezing tightly on the head of the penis. If you are strong enough, you can even squeeze so tightly that he can't remove his penis from you. You may enjoy this sexual control over your partner, though be careful; it's possible for a woman with very strong PC muscles to hurt her partner by literally squeezing too hard. Rhythmic grasping and releasing of the penis to "milk" it is particularly erotic at the point of his orgasm.

✻ ✻ The Male Kegels ✻ ✻

The muscles the man wants to exercise are in the area of the *cremaster* and *pubococcygeal* muscles. Here's how to locate the muscle group involved. Focus your physical "awareness" on the base of the penis and the rectal area; squeeze these muscles as if you were trying to draw your testicles close to your body. Or imagine that you are trying to siphon water up through your penis into your bladder—a sort of reverse urination. Or contract the muscles that are used to start or stop the flow of urination.

You should be able to locate these muscles fairly easily, though you may find that initially you are not able to contract the muscles very well. It's probably a very weak contraction, and nothing will seem to move very far. That's okay, it'll change with exercise. You might also try doing these exercises with an erection; it's easier to feel the muscles then, and will probably help you get used to working them.

Now, squeeze and relax these muscles ten times in a row; when you first start the exercises, hold for a second or two, then relax for a second or two, then repeat, and so on. At first you may not be able to hold for even a second; you'll find that the muscle contracts but then seems to relax itself without any command to do so from you. Later, you'll be able to hold the contraction for five, ten, or fifteen seconds. Continue these exercises each day, gradually increasing the number of contractions and the length of contraction. For instance, you might aim for forty to sixty contractions a day, holding them for five or six seconds at a time.

Get into the habit of doing these exercises at a particular time or during a particular activity. You might do them while shaving or driving to work, for instance. You can exercise these internal muscles without breaking a sweat!

✻ ✻ Using the PC Muscles ✻ ✻

Strengthening the PC muscles provides the man with a number of benefits. First, it provides a sort of psychological boost. The penis feels somehow larger, more powerful, the erection harder. You can rhythmically throb the penis inside your lover when you are not thrusting. She'll enjoy the feeling of your penis growing and filling her vagina, and may even find that it rubs against the G spot. (We'll discuss the G spot more in Module 28.) You'll have better orgasmic control—you'll be able to hold back more easily. And you might try pulsing the muscles when you orgasm for an unusual sensation.

Sexual Position #1

Most of the modules in this book contain suggested sexual positions. We've put these in to help you add a little variety to your sex life—try something different! In most cases, though not all, the position at the end of the module is related in some way to what we've discussed during the module; and the very first position we'll look at is related to the power of Kegel exercises.

The *Kama Sutra* talks of a position in which the woman "acts the part of a man" (that is, she is on top), and in which she "holds the lingam in her yoni, draws it in, presses it, and keeps it thus in her for a long time." This position is called the "pair of tongs."

She can sit upright, as shown, and use the strength of her PC muscles to clutch his penis and rhythmically massage it with her vagina. She may be able to direct his penis to massage her G spot, and can use her hands to stimulate her clitoris. Combine this with gentle movement of the hips, growing to more vigorous action as the excitement builds.

Module 2

Fit for Life, Fit for Sex

It doesn't matter if you are young or old, fat or thin, a college professor or a teenage high-school student, in perfect health or not so healthy, you've probably been interested in sex from the time you first discovered your genitals. Most likely you want to make it better, too—after all, you bought this book! You've read other books and magazine articles about how to enhance your sex life, you may have been convinced that sex is an equal-opportunity entertainment—all that counts is your psychological attitude, right? Learn a few new tricks, and off you go.

The way you think about sex is an essential aspect of sexual enjoyment, it's true. But consider this, who turns you on more? A person who is fit and trim, or one who is flabby and bulging? We all, at least occasionally, look at people we've only just met with sexual thoughts in our minds . . . but how often do you meet someone who's in atrocious physical condition and think, "Wow, let's get physical!" Not often, we'll bet. But the physical-fitness component is a two-way street. Not only do you find people more sexually appealing if they are physically fit (and, of course, others will look at you with the same bias), but have you noticed just how much *work* sex can be when you are out of condition?

Most sex advice completely ignores physical condition and focuses on the psychological and physical aspects of the sexual act itself. It's certainly true that almost anyone can enjoy sex, and it's also true that what you *think* about sex is extremely important. But when you get right down to it, sex is a *physical* act. It's all very well to get hung up on the psychological aspects, but you can go too far, as British journalist Malcolm Muggeridge considered when talking about sex and the English: "It has to be admitted," he said, "that we English have sex on the brain, which is a very unsatisfactory place to have it."

You see, it's a simple biological fact that (contrary to popular myth), sex is *not* all in the mind. The fitter you are, the better sex can be, for two reasons. First, sex is a physical activity and, just as with skiing, swimming, or hiking, the fitter you are the better you will perform. (And the better you perform, the more fun, for both you and your partner.) Also, your physical condition affects your mental condition. Fit people tend to be more optimistic, happy, and energetic. The fitter you are the more likely you are to look forward to sex, the more eager to initiate sex, and the more willing to say "Yes!" when your partner suggests getting physical. So while sex can be enjoyed by almost anyone, it will be enjoyed more—and more often—by those in good physical condition.

One of us (Dr. James White) has made a lifetime study of exercise and sex and the link between the two. He notes his credentials and his findings as follows: Over a period of thirty years at the University of California, San Diego, I have taught Anatomy and Physiology in the Department of Physical Education, and was the Director of Exercise Physiology and the Human Performance Laboratory. I also taught at the UCSD School of Medicine. I was an elected fellow of the American College of Sports Medicine, and have been a member of the National Collegiate Athletic Association (NCAA) and American Heart Association, and on the committee of the National Collegiate Fencing Association. I've served on the faculty of the Scripps Clinic in La Jolla, California, and have been an Olympic fencing coach. My work has appeared in the *New England Journal of Medicine;* in *Chest;* in *Medicine and Science in Sports and Exercise,* and in other journals. That's my "exercise" resume. On top of that I've been, at various times, a member of the San Diego Society for Sex Therapy and Education and The Society for the Scientific Study of Sex. I'm a Board Certified Sex Researcher (with the title of Diplomate), with the American Board of Sexology. My work has also appeared in the *Archives of Sexual Behavior,* and other journals. So I've studied exercise, I've studied sex, and I've seen how the two are linked. But this theory isn't simply personal opinion. I have hard facts to back up these claims.

Part of my work was collaborating in research at the Veterans Administration Hospital in San Diego, helping men and women of all ages learn about their bodies and become physically fit. During that work we heard so many complaints about sexual problems, from so many of our study subjects, that we decided to find out how serious these problems were, and to see if we could discover a remedy. During the next fifteen years we screened and interviewed over 5,000 men, analyzing their physical health in 22 different areas. We used what we learned to create a base line, then continued with a nine-month program of exercise, nutritional guidance, stress reduction, and help to quit smoking. The results were dramatic. The men who followed the program became fitter, of course. But that's not all. Here's what else they experienced:

- They desired sex more often.
- They had sex more often.
- They were more sexually responsive to their partners, and more easily turned on.
- They fantasized about sex more frequently.
- They had fewer sexual problems and performance failures.
- They were more satisfied with all aspects of their sex lives.

We studied men—it's very difficult to get money to study sexuality, and the major reason our study was funded was that at the time there was a lot of interest in discovering how men can avoid heart attacks. The sexuality part of the study was a sort of "bonus."

Still, for the past five years we've been collecting data on women and the effect of diet and exercise on their sexuality. Although we're not quite ready to publish our data, we are sure of one thing: As with men, there are real sexual benefits for women to be fit. Now, in some ways sexual benefits are much easier to measure with men. If a man is impotent due to poor physical health, for instance, that's a solid statistic. With women the sexual benefits of good health and the sexual problems due to poor health are often more subtle— simple lack of desire, for instance. If a man can't get an erection, he'll often avoid sex. If a woman can't orgasm, or just isn't interested in sex, she may still have sex to please her mate.

All in all, though, we believe there's no question of the relationship between health and sexuality for women—the healthier the woman, the more interested in sex she's likely to be. She tends to be more confident. She has better self-esteem, and feels better about her appearance. And as with men, her testosterone levels are likely to be higher, increasing her level of sexual desire.

If we could bottle and sell this, we'd make a fortune. Imagine something that makes you feel better, live longer . . . and have better sex! But that's just what getting into shape can do for you.

You'll feel better—both in and out of bed. By the way, the conclusions reached by this study are borne out by several subsequent studies. The simple, incontestable fact is that fitter people have better sex. If you improve your health, you'll also improve your sex.

So what do you need to do to improve your sex life by improving your health? We've all heard so much over the past decade or two about getting into shape—about improving our diet, exercising more, avoiding certain drugs, and so on. There's a wealth of information on this subject, and we don't have room to duplicate it here. But we'd like to quickly go over the main ways that you can get fitter and gain sexual benefits as a wonderful bonus. In the rest of this module we're going to discuss how exercise can help—and how stress can hurt—your sex life. Then, in the next chapter, we'll look at the role of diet and drugs in your sex life.

✷ ✷ Exercise—Feel Better, in More Ways Than One ✷ ✷

In the mid-1970s we at the Exercise Physiology and Human Performance Laboratory at the University of California, San Diego, embarked on a study to see if lifestyle changes would improve male sexuality. We examined a group of middle-aged, economically successful business executives. We tested every organ and looked into every body orifice we could find. We checked blood pressure, heart rate, cardiac capacity, muscle strength, and body fat. We then put them on a ten-week exercise and nutrition program. Not surprisingly, they became healthier. Perhaps more surprising was their response to questions about their sex lives. Men who had claimed they were "frequently" or "occasionally" sexually frustrated now claimed that they were "hardly ever" frustrated.

In a follow-up study, cosponsored by the Veterans Administration Hospital in La Jolla, California, we put 80 men between the ages of 32 and 62 on an exercise and nutrition program and asked them to keep records of their sexual activities. What did we find? As the program progressed and the men became fitter, they reported that they became sexually aroused more often. They also had orgasms more frequently—and the orgasms were more intense.

In the years that followed we studied over 5,000 men. Some were assigned to keep diaries recording their sexual feelings and behavior during a nine-month period. We also followed a "control" group, a group of men who kept a sexual-activity diary, but who made no changes in exercise or diet. Then, in the summer of 1990 we published our results in the *Archives of Sexual Behavior.*

We found, of course, that the men who underwent the exercise program and improved their diet, also improved their health. They had lower blood pressure, lower total cholesterol levels, greater muscle mass, less body fat, and improvements in every physiological measure. But we also found important sexual changes we suspected might occur:

- The subjects on the exercise and diet program became sexually aroused more often than the control group.
- The subjects on the exercise/diet program initiated more kissing and caressing with their partners than the control group, and had fewer

periods of low sex drive.

- As the program progressed, the subjects in the exercise/diet group had sexual intercourse and orgasms about 30 percent more often than the "old-habits" group.

- These subjects fantasized about sex more than the control group.

- All this fantasizing had an interesting side effect . . . the exercisers masturbated more frequently than before, 50 percent more, in fact. (Hey, what's wrong with that? As world-famous sexologist Woody Allen said about masturbation, "Don't knock it, it's sex with someone you love.")

Not all of the exercisers experienced great change in their sexual lives, though. The few that continued smoking did not increase the frequency of intercourse, orgasm, and fantasizing nearly as much as those who stopped smoking.

✳ ✳ So Why Does It Work? ✳ ✳

Why does exercise improve sex? There are several reasons.

- Exercise increases the level of testosterone in the body, which helps both men and women. This potent hormone breaks down glycogen, providing a quick source of energy for the body. Testosterone also fuels a man's sex drive. Moderate exercise also seems to increase testosterone levels in women's bodies, too, increasing sex drive.

- Exercise and a low-fat diet will improve circulation. (In men, blood vessels clogged by cholesterol can lead to erectile problems—if arteries cannot supply blood to the penis, the penis cannot enlarge adequately.)

- Exercise can also improve blood flow and oxygen pickup. Your heart pumps more blood for each beat, and your breathing becomes deeper and more forceful, allowing the blood to take more oxygen to the muscles.

- You'll have more energy for *all* activities—including sex.

- The fitter you are, the more confident you are likely to be. Studies showing that exercise and diet improve overall confidence abound, but in what area is self-confidence more important than sex? You'll look better, and feel better about the way you look. And the better you look and feel, the more responsive your partner is likely to be!

- The healthier you are, the better you'll look; the more appealing you'll be to your partner. As British journalist Katherine Whitehorn once said, "Outside every thin woman is a fat man trying to get in." (Hopefully the fat man will consider a diet and exercise program, too.)

We are not alone in our conclusions. Our results have been confirmed by other researchers. Phillip Whitten (a Harvard University expert on human behavioral biology), and his research assistant, Elizabeth Whiteside, studied

160 competitive swimmers, one group in their forties and the other in their fifties. Each person swam, on average, about an hour a day, four or five days a week.

"Our study clearly demonstrates that regular exercise can improve your love life," Whitten and Whiteside said in an article on their findings published in the April 1989 issue of *Psychology Today*. "The men and women in our study reported sex lives more like those of people in their twenties and thirties than those of their contemporaries. Not only that, but those in their sixties reported sex lives comparable to those in their forties."

⋇ ⋇ The Exercise Regimen ⋇ ⋇

What awful exercise regimen do you need to undergo? Nothing particularly arduous. Yes, you need to sweat now and again, but you don't need to get into marathon-running condition. In fact, exercise that is too intense can reverse the desired effect, *reducing* sex drive. In our study, for instance, most of the men did not regard themselves as athletes, and you don't need to be one to reap sexual benefits from exercise. You simply need to get into the habit of doing moderately vigorous physical activity several times a week, along with a sensible diet. We found that the men in our study who exercised vigorously four to six days a week were healthier and had more orgasms than men who exercised less. Men who exercised significantly more, however—running over 240 minutes each week or bicycling over 250 miles a week, for instance—might become extremely fit and strong, but were likely to experience a drop in sexual activity.

Take a look at the following chart. It shows what we found in our study—

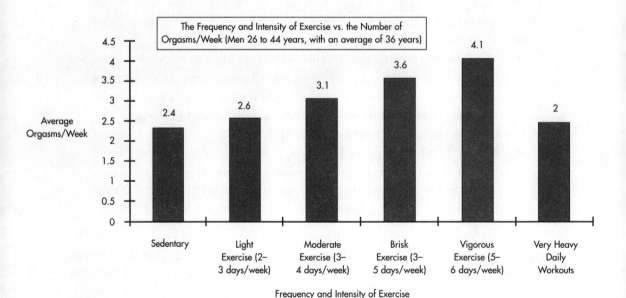

that the number of orgasms the men in our study had each week was related to the frequency and intensity of exercise.

You can see from this chart a dramatic drop in sexual activity for those superfit men; they actually have *less* sex than the couch potatoes! So it's not necessary to prepare for the Ironman contest to improve your sex life; even quite moderate exercise will help.

✻ ✻ Sex as Exercise ✻ ✻

Isn't sex itself exercise? Yes, and perhaps the most fun form. It may not be as effective for improving your overall physical fitness as, say, running, biking, or swimming, but depending on the amount of effort you put into it, it can be on a par with walking. Still, if you want to give your partner *another* reason for having sex, beyond the normal ones that we all know so well, you could point out that sex does burn calories. If you've got a choice of playing couch potato and having sex, you're definitely better off with the latter form of entertainment. The following table shows you how many calories you are likely to burn:

Calories Burned Per Minute (Above the Normal Resting Rate of Calorie Consumption) During Sex

Weight	Intensity of Sexual Activity					
	Hugging/ Kissing	Foreplay	Active Foreplay	Active Sex	Vigorous Sex	Extremely Vigorous Sex
110	0.6	1.8	2.4	2.5	3.6	4.2–6.0
125	0.7	2.1	2.8	2.9	4.2	4.9–7.0
150	1.0	3.0	3.8	4.2	5.8	7.1–9.5
165	1.1	3.3	4.1	4.5	6.5	7.6–10
175	1.2	3.6	4.8	4.9	7.2	8.4–11
185	1.3	3.8	5.0	5.2	7.9	8.8–12
195	1.4	4.0	5.3	5.5	8.2	9.2–13
210	1.5	4.3	5.7	5.9	8.6	9.8–14
230	1.8	4.9	6.6	7.2	9.0	11–15

For example, during casual foreplay a 150-pound man or woman will burn about three calories per minute; as the session progresses and he or she gets involved in vigorous intercourse, that will increase to almost six calories per minute. So during 20 minutes of lovemaking this person could burn about, oh, maybe 80 or 90 calories. Not a lot, but every little bit counts. Add it up during a year of lovemaking, and you could burn enough calories to lose three to five pounds of fat.

You'll notice from this chart that the leaner you are, the fewer calories a particular activity will burn. That means that, as you become fitter and lose weight, having sex will burn fewer calories. Our advice? Have sex more often, more vigorously, and for a longer time to make up for it. Indeed, our studies suggest you probably will anyway, with or without our advice.

Finally, a warning. Don't be deceived by the likes of Sophia Loren, who said it doesn't matter much what you look like. "Sex appeal is 50 percent what you've got and 50 percent what people think you've got," she claimed. Easy to say, when you've got what she's got! So take *our* advice, and make the *most* of what you've got.

✄ ✄ Stress— Sex-Drive Assassin ✄ ✄

If you've ever suffered from serious stress, you know how debilitating it can be, and how disinterested in sex it makes you. Stress and anxiety are the two main inhibitors of sexual arousal. Normal sexual impulses that flow to the genitals are inhibited by stress and anxiety. In men erection is inhibited, and in women the symptoms are reduced desire coupled with diminished vaginal lubrication.

Stress causes a message to be sent to a part of the brain called the hypothalamus, which sends messages to the autonomic nervous system (to shut down the sexual reflex system) and to the pituitary gland. The pituitary gland tells the adrenal and other glands to produce a variety of hormones, chemical stimulators for organs throughout the body. These hormones get the body ready to fight. After all, if you are under stress, the body figures it must be under attack. Blood vessels constrict, increasing blood pressure; heart rate increases, and each heartbeat is strengthened, so the heart pumps more blood; the blood thickens; sugar in the liver is released to make more energy available; and blood is moved away from the digestive system, so it's ready for use by the muscles.

Of course, if you are about to go into battle, the last thing you need is sex; you should be watching out for imminent attack, not thinking about having fun. So the body also diverts blood from the genitals, reducing them in size; draws the penis and testicles up close to the body, to protect them; and inhibits the normal sexual response—erections, sexual fantasies, and all kinds of sexual thoughts are "turned off."

That's fine if this is a short-term event, and you really do have a threat that you should be dealing with right away. But long-term stress can cause your body to act as if it's *continually* under threat of assault. Apart from harming your overall health, it continuously ruins your sex life.

If you suffer from stress and anxiety that's so bad it affects your sex life, you need to do something about it! Not just to rescue your sex life, but to save your life, as well. High levels of stress can lead to heart disease, asthma, alcoholism, and much more. So how can you deal with stress?

- Start an exercise program right away, even if you haven't yet decided what's causing your stress. Exercise is one of the very best ways to reduce stress; it feels as if you are burning the stress away, and in a very real chemical sense you are; you are reducing the level of epinephrine in your body (the stress hormone), and increasing the level of endorphins (the body's natural tranquilizers).
- Make sure you are eating properly. A poor diet can contribute to stress, a good diet can help protect you from it.
- Avoid coffee and other caffeinated drinks; these will just heighten your stress.
- Avoid alcohol; while it may temporarily anesthetize you, in the long term it will depress you and make your stress worse.
- Try to figure out what is causing your stress. Is it your job? Are you fighting with your partner? Are you in debt and going deeper? Once you've found the cause, do what it takes to resolve the problem. Find another job or somehow change your work situation. See a marriage counselor. Talk with a financial counselor and work out a plan to pay off your debts.
- Take meditation, deep-relaxation, or biofeedback classes. These techniques can bring about dramatic improvements in your levels of stress and anxiety, by teaching your body to deal with the stress factors in a different manner.

Dealing with stress is a serious issue, and not one to be taken lightly. Speak with your doctor, read a few books on the subject, and get involved in finding a way to deal with the problem. You—and your partner—will be happier for it.

Module 3

You Are What You Eat (and Smoke, and Drink . . .)

Over the past few years—past few decades, really—we've heard so much about why we should improve our diets that many people are fed up with it (if you'll excuse the pun). For all the talk, American diets are not improving greatly. Sugar and fat consumption has actually *increased,* for instance. Clearly people may *talk* about eating better, but when it comes time to actually eat properly, theory doesn't seem to have much effect on practice.

You've heard that you should improve your diet to keep your weight down, to maintain proper cholesterol levels (the good cholesterol high, the bad one low), to avoid high blood pressure and heart disease, and so on. But how often have you heard a report on the evening news telling you that if you eat well you'll enjoy sex more? How often have you read an article telling you that if you eat well you may even enjoy sex more *often?*

Well, it's true. We found in our lab that properly fed people are sexually active people. Does diet directly affect your sex life? Absolutely!

- When overweight people reduce their weight their sexual interest grows, and they are more easily aroused. A great reason to get into shape yourself, and to encourage your partner to become fit, too.
- When overweight people become trim, they tend to have sexual intercourse and orgasms more often.
- Slim down and your partner will find you more attractive.

- You know that "I'm-so-stuffed-I-can-hardly-move" feeling experienced after a meal? How often do you feel like sex when you're stuffed with food? (This is of special concern to a man—blood is diverted to digesting the meal, so one thing that *won't* be stuffed is his erection!)
- Many Americans suffer from hypoglycemia, symptoms caused by high sugar consumption. One of the symptoms is a reduced sex drive, but the other symptoms won't help you feel sexy, either—nervousness, irritability, headaches.
- Just how sexy do you feel when constipated or when suffering from hemorrhoids? (More fiber and Vitamin C in your diet will help.)

Our study found a strong relationship between cholesterol levels and sexual activity. We found that, up to a certain point, the higher the levels of HDL, the more orgasms our subjects experienced. (HDL is High Density Lipoprotein, the "good" cholesterol. HDL tends to reduce cholesterol deposition on artery walls, and actually clear out previous accumulations.) You can see this relationship in the following chart. Note that men with the highest HDL levels also had fewer orgasms than men with slightly lower rates. These men are involved in extremely rigorous athletic training—many are triathletes and Ironman competitors—which tends to reduce sexual activity.

We're not suggesting that HDL levels have a direct effect on sexual function, of course. Rather, they are an indicator of an overall level of health that leads to improved sexual function. It's not a cause and effect, it's a correlation, we're saying. People who exercise more tend to have higher HDL levels and they also tend to be more sexually active. People who are overweight are unlikely to have high HDL levels, and people who are overweight also have lower testosterone levels. This leads, in both men and women, to reduced sexual desire.

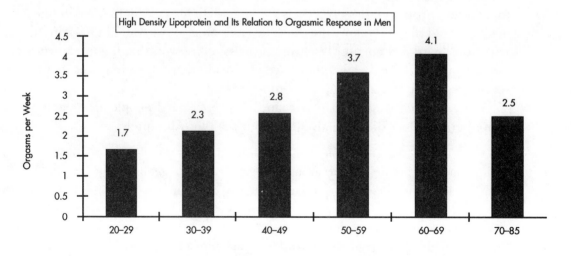

High Density Lipoprotein and Its Relation to Orgasmic Response in Men

High Density Lipoprotein (mg%)

This isn't a diet book. But there again, most diets are notoriously ineffective anyway. Studies have shown that most fad dieters—83 percent of them—regain all their lost weight within six to nine months, and that within two years an astounding 97 percent of them are heavier than their original weight! Instead, we're going to provide you with a few simple guidelines to sensible eating. It's really not hard to eat well if you are willing to make a few reasonable changes. Don't try to lose more than four to five pounds per month and don't worry about counting every calorie. So here are a few sensible suggestions:

1. **Don't Overeat!** Avoid what's known as the *Last Supper Syndrome,* the tendency to fill your plate as if it will be the last plate of food you'll ever eat. You know what we mean . . . how often do you finish a meal and have to loosen your belt? Or perhaps you lean back, take a deep breath, and tell the others at the table that you're "stuffed." There's really no need to eat like this.

2. **Don't Skip Meals** While missing a meal now and again might seem a good way to avoid a few calories, it's a double-edged sword. Extending the time between meals can cause your blood-sugar levels to drop to the degree that you suffer from hypoglycemic symptoms—irritability, shakiness, insecurity, depression, tiredness, loss of sexual desire, sugar craving, and increased appetite. Not only won't you feel good, you may end up eating more, and the wrong type of food, too. Even if you manage to last from one meal all the way to the next without snacking, you'll quite likely gorge yourself at the next meal.

3. **Throw Out the Salt Shaker** You *don't* need to add salt to your food, either while cooking or on the plate. Why? Because there's more than enough salt already in our food; while you only need one to two grams of salt a day, most people get between ten and twenty grams a day! Too much salt increases water retention, which leads to elevated blood pressure. Increased blood pressure also speeds the rate of deposition of cholesterol on the arteries, resulting in diminished blood supply to the genitals.

4. **Up the Fiber** Make sure you get enough dietary fiber (roughage) in your diet. Fiber binds and holds fat in the intestine, keeping it away from your liver—where it would be converted to cholesterol, which then finds its way onto your arteries. Fiber also hastens removal of waste materials from the intestines more quickly (you probably know that fiber helps "cure" constipation), and this quick removal eliminates cancer-causing substances in the lower bowel. You'll feel better, and you'll halve your chance of getting bowel cancer, and reduce the chance of getting colon and rectal cancer, too.

5. **Sugar** Most Americans eat too much sugar. For all the talk about the dangers of sugar over the past twenty years, sugar consumption has actually

increased! According to Dr. Robert C. Atkins, M.D., a well-known "diet doctor," author, and doctor of complementary medicine, average sugar consumption has increased from 118 pounds per person per year in 1978 to 139 pounds in 1989.

What's wrong with sugar? Almost one-third of heavy sugar eaters have hypoglycemic symptoms—nervousness, loss of attention, fatigue, reduced productivity . . . and diminished sex drive. You might think that eating lots of sugar will give you lots of energy, but the opposite is often true; because your body can't manufacture adequate insulin to handle the sugar overload, your blood-sugar level yo-yos, ending up too low.

6. **Reduce Fats** Within five hours of eating a fatty meal, the diameter of your arteries will constrict—the arteries in the eyes become twenty-five percent smaller, for instance. Arteries throughout your body will become constricted—including to your penis, if you have one. Over the long term, high-fat diets are believed to cause semi-permanent blood-vessel constriction. Semi-permanent, because the constriction can be reversed by modifying the diet.

   We found that on average, forty-five percent to fifty-five percent of all the calories consumed by the men in our study came from fats! Current guidelines suggest that over thirty percent is probably too much. We reduced this amount to twenty percent to twenty-five percent. In particular you are interested in reducing *saturated* fats. These are fats that are solid at room temperature, and they are found in whole milk, ice cream, fatty cheeses, lard, butter, egg yolks, fatty meats (pork, beef, duck), and hydrogenated vegetable oils, such as palm and coconut oil.

7. **Eat More Vegetables** Eating a lot of vegetables is important. They provide you with the roughage you need, plenty of vitamins and other cancer-fighting nutrients, and decrease your cholesterol levels. And when you eat vegetables you are providing your body with the nutrients it needs in a beneficial form, rather than providing them mixed in with simple sugars, fats, and excess protein. Try increasing the vegetable portions on your plate, and reducing the meat.

❀ ❀ Drugs— Don't Deaden Your Sexuality ❀ ❀

Another thing to consider is the effect of drugs on your sexuality. Virtually all of us take drugs of some kind, whether doctor-prescribed medicines, over-the-counter remedies, or legal and illegal recreational drugs. And many of these substances can dramatically reduce sexual potential.

✣ ✣ You Can Drink Caffeine, But . . . ✣ ✣

People survived millennia without coffee . . . believe it or not; coffee is not a major food group, though we know some people who act as if it is. Dump the coffee, and improve your sex life. Or at least consider cutting down a little, and avoiding it at certain times of day. Caffeine—whether from coffee, tea, or soft drinks—accelerates blood pressure and heart rate, and has been implicated in elevated cholesterol levels. Some reports suggest that coffee can cause coronary heart disease; a study of coffee drinkers at the Johns Hopkins School of Medicine found that coffee drinkers had two to three times as many coronary "episodes" as nonimbibers. Caffeine has been linked to breast cancer in women, too.

Here's another reason to cut down or quit; according to a study in a mental clinic, the more caffeine consumed, the more likely a person is to suffer from depression, anxiety, personality disorders, learning dysfunction, and even psychoses. Ah, we can hear you saying, what good is a study like that in a mental hospital, of *course* these people are suffering from mental illnesses! The researchers replaced the coffee with a decaffeinated brand of coffee—without informing the staff or patients—and the patients improved so dramatically that the hospital eventually banned caffeine.

There is a direct sexual link, too. Zinc is known to power your sex drive. Caffeine, however, hinders the absorption of zinc into the genital area. Caffeine also lowers Vitamin B levels and normal blood-sugar levels, leading to heartburn and associated problems. Caffeine has been linked to lumpy and painful breasts. If you drink more than two cups of coffee a day, you should try taking a Vitamin E supplement, as it may reduce the lumps and pain. Oh, and if you miss a cup of coffee that you'd normally have, you'll experience caffeine withdrawal. ("Not tonight, dear, I have a headache." Sound familiar?)

If you want to try quitting coffee, try taking vitamin C; a Czechoslovakian researcher gave 150 mg of vitamin C to people trying to quit coffee and found that they became more alert, and had fewer accidents. Later research found greater improvement with about one gram a day.

✣ ✣ The Marlboro Man's Dirty Little Secret ✣ ✣

How can it be that a habit associated with burning and ash and breath from hell has become linked in many people's minds with sex? Smoking has long been seen as something sensual. Movies often depicted smoking as something seductive and arousing. Of course the tobacco companies have spent many billions of dollars over the past century pushing smoking as a sophisticated thing to do and, as any good advertising executive will tell you, sex sells; many of the millions of different ads the world has been subjected to have subtly— and sometimes not so subtly—linked smoking with sex.

At one time the tobacco companies claimed that smoking was good for you. Nobody believes that now, and we know for sure something else—that smoking's not good for sex, either. In fact, the more you smoke, the more likely you are to have sexual problems. A fifty-year-old man who smokes is two to three times more likely to be impotent than nonsmokers of his age. In older smokers, erectile problems are quite frequent. And, as you can see from the following chart, the more a man smokes, the more problems he will have. The chart is based on men with an average age of 44.9 years (ranging from 29 to 65 years).

Many of these studies have been done on men, but preliminary information from some of our pilot studies suggests that there are sexual benefits when women give up smoking. We all know that smoking's bad for us, men and women but, as with men, women can obtain sexual benefits by avoiding tobacco. The differences for women are often more subtle, though. Male smokers can become impotent. Women smokers may simply lose desire— their poor health leads to reduced interest in sex. We've also noted, from one of our pilot studies on women and sex, that when a woman stops smoking her *partner* becomes more interested in sex. A woman who quits tobacco is likely

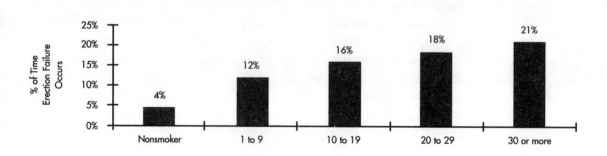

How Smoking Relates to the Frequency of Erectile Dysfunction

% of Time Erection Failure Occurs

Number of Cigarettes Smoked Each Day

The Best Sex of Your Life

to enjoy more passionate kissing, and her mate is more inclined to be sexually intimate. Now, the pilot study was quite small, but we still believe there's a really strong trend here.

What causes these problems? A research group at Queens College in Kingston, Ontario, studied 178 impotent men, and found that the smokers had reduced blood flow to the penis. Nicotine constricts the caliber of the arteries, and causes increased cholesterol to be laid onto the inside of the arteries, reducing the cross-sectional area through which the blood flows. The arteries become smaller "pipes," so less blood can get through to the erectile chambers.

The Marlboro Man looks good, but can't deliver. In our studies we found that smokers are less interested in intercourse and oral sex than nonsmokers—but that's okay, they don't have intercourse or oral sex or orgasms as much as nonsmokers, anyway. They are also less able to get a second erection and orgasm within thirty minutes of the first orgasm than nonsmokers. Overall, we believe that nonsmokers desire and acquire nearly twice as much sexual activity as smokers their own age.

How about cigars? They're sophisticated, they're currently very much in vogue, and *they're still very harmful.* It's true that cigar smokers often have fewer physiological problems than smokers—unless they used to be cigarette smokers, in which case they are likely to inhale. But we've found that cigar smokers get fewer kisses than both nonsmokers *and* cigarette smokers! Their mates are often turned off by the lingering smell.

One more thing, before we move on to other drugs . . . a quick word about that great smoker's tradition, a cigarette in bed after sex. This little ritual actually contributes to detumescence—that's penile shrinking after sex, in less technical language. The smoker takes more time to get another erection, and when (or if) he actually gets one, it's likely to be less rigid than a nonsmoker's erection.

By the way, all this talk of rigid penises, and the speed of erections, and so on . . . how do we know all this? Who, exactly, measures this stuff? ("I want that job," I can hear some women shouting!) Well, there's something called a *photoplethysmograph* which is strapped onto the penis and measures changes in the diameter of the penis, the rate of growth of the penis, and the length of time that the erection lasts. Now, D. G. Gilbert carried out experiments using these things with a group of men. Each man had one of these odd devices strapped onto his staff of life, and was either sitting watching pornographic movies, or sitting watching porn movies while smoking! Gilbert could then compare penile responses of the smoking group against those of the nonsmoking group. This is probably not the sort of job Mrs. Gilbert had in mind for her son when he was a young lad, but it's interesting stuff nonetheless.

❧ ❧ Other Drugs ❧ ❧

Cigarettes are likely the most commonly used substance that reduces sexual function, but there are plenty more, drugs of many kinds. Legal and illegal, recreational and medicinal, over-the-counter and by prescription, drugs of many kinds cause sexual problems. There are many ways that drugs can hurt your overall health—and, in turn, your sex life. But let's see a few ways that recreational drugs *directly* damage your sexual performance.

- **Stimulants—Amphetamines and Cocaine:** Users often can't achieve a feeling of sexual satisfaction. Long-term amphetamine and cocaine use can cause prostate disorders and permanently inhibited ejaculation. Withdrawing from these stimulants leads to a variety of symptoms including a total loss of interest in sex.
- **Marijuana:** This drug affects the endocrine system, reducing the amount of testosterone in the body; less than one joint can cut levels enough to decrease sexual interest. Although one user in three claims that smoking pot improves sex, studies show that it generally leads to sexual apathy and an inability to climax. Heavy smokers become generally disinterested in sex, and men may develop erectile problems, even impotence.
- **Alcohol:** Reduces testosterone levels and the hardness of erections (thus the term, *brewer's droop*). In men, and more particularly in women, as little as one drink of alcohol can block the ability to reach orgasm.
- **Opiates—Heroin, Morphine, Opium, Methadone:** The opiates "lock on" to receptors in the brain's pleasure centers and the sexual arousal centers of the nervous system. Many users experience a total loss of interest in sex for several days. Sexual fantasies and dreams as well as a man's morning erections disappear. About half of all heroin addicts are able to indulge in nothing more than what's known to addicts as "fucking with a dead stick"; they can maintain an erection for an extended period, and thrust for a long time . . . but not achieve orgasm.
- **Anabolic Steroids:** How ironic that a drug used by many men to build their bodies into temples of machismo, also shrinks their balls. They'll also suffer from diminished sperm count, and decreased sex drive. On top of that, they often become very angry and aggressive . . . and may get acne. Real sex machines, eh?

Oh, here's another way that illegal drugs can hurt your sex life; you'll find that your sexual choices are very limited in jail! (And usually not particularly desirable, either.)

✷ ✷ Problems in Your Medicine Cabinet ✷ ✷

It's not only recreational drugs that can harm your sex drive and function. Many medicinal drugs, both over-the-counter and prescription, can hurt you too. In fact, if you are suffering from some kind of sexual dysfunction, and are regularly taking a medicinal drug, ask your doctor or pharmacist if the drug has sexual side effects, or take a look in *The Physician's Desk Reference,* which you can find in many pharmacies and libraries. Drugs used to treat hypertension, psychiatric problems, ulcers, and so on, often cause sexual problems—delayed or inhibited orgasm, decreased libido, erectile problems, impotence, and so on. Even over-the-counter antihistamines, anti-inflammatories, and decongestants can cause problems.

If you think you may be taking a drug that is hurting your sex life, talk with your doctor. Ask if there's another drug you can try, or whether you might try reducing the dosage. And ask about nondrug therapies, too, such as diet and exercise. You may not be able to drop the offending drug right away, but you may be able to start a long-term program that will eventually free you from that medication.

✷ ✷ What About Aphrodisiacs? ✷ ✷

How about aphrodisiacs, drugs (and certain foods) that are supposed to increase sexual desire and ability? There's some bad news and some good news. The bad news is that virtually all of the substances sold as or purported to be aphrodisiacs—Spanish Fly (which is actually the pulverized thorax of a particular form of beetle), raw oysters, chocolate, the gall bladder of a bear, the penis of a tiger, and so on—*don't* work. And in many cases these substances are dangerous—they sometimes cause sickness, occasionally even death. (Have *you* ever tried to remove the loins from a crocodile or the penis from a tiger?)

While anecdotal evidence may suggest this substance or that works as an aphrodisiac, scientific experiments almost always show that it *doesn't* work. (A possible exception is *yohimbe;* some experiments have shown that yohimbe, a substance taken from the bark of a West African tree, does act as an aphrodisiac, although other experiments suggest that it doesn't.) Why the difference between anecdote and science? People who take aphrodisiacs are invariably thinking about sex when they do so. Spend an hour or two thinking about sex, anticipating the sex you are about to have, hoping for results from a substance designed to get you turned on . . . and the chances are, you'll get pretty horny. That's not chemistry, that's psychology.

Now the good news; there is a scientifically proven aphrodisiac, and it's widely available. It's called "a balanced diet full of food that's good for you." Eat well—and get some exercise, too—and you won't need a drug of some form to stimulate you sexually. You'll be turned on and ready to go without any additional help.

Module 4

Keeping Sexual Excitement Alive

Perhaps the major sexual problem experienced by couples is that of differing sexual appetites. One partner wants more sex than the other. One wants oral sex, the other doesn't. The man is tired of having to always ask for sex, while the woman feels it's his job to initiate. It's quite understandable that sexual incompatibility is common—after all, sex is such a weird and wonderful thing that it's hard to imagine how two people could like exactly the same games.

Early in most relationships this isn't much of a problem. Couples tend to have so much sex and so much variety at the beginning of their relationship that differences in desire don't become obvious. It's often later in the relationship, as sex becomes more routine and mundane, that these problems arise. The secret to dealing with sexual incompatibility is often to revive sex, to keep the sexual spark in the relationship. And it's possible for couples to come closer to compatibility, if they simply understand the desires and needs of their partners, and make an effort to accommodate those needs and desires.

✤ ✤ A Few Ways to Keep the Excitement Going ✤ ✤

As your relationship matures, sex will probably become less exciting. That's a simple fact of life, something that's been proven by study, by survey, and by polls. But there are ways to maintain the excitement. Here are a few basic principles (the rest of the book provides the actual practice!):

- Avoid the "sexual rut" by making it a rule that you never repeat exactly the same sexual routine twice in a row.
- Make sure you tell each other what you enjoy, what you fantasize about, and what you'd like to try. Perhaps you could have a discussion night once every few weeks, in which you talk about the things you'd like to do to each other—and then do them.
- Don't relegate sex to nighttime. The night is in some ways the worst time you can have sex: You're often exhausted, distracted, sometimes inebriated. Why not have sex in the morning? When he wakes up with an erection, use it. Or during the day; after lunch on the weekend have a little nap, then wake up and make love. Why not make love *before* you go out in the evening—it'll probably be more exciting than when you come back tired and the worse for food and drink.

Be More Romantic

A question for the man: Do you recall when you were eager for sex to the point of distraction and attempted to seduce a woman? It's quite likely that whatever you said or did, you weren't successful. The woman probably felt your urgency; it made her uncomfortable, she didn't trust you, and she didn't respond.

A better method might be to calm down and stay friendly. You want to show your authentic self, you want to be natural and calm—not bouncing off the walls like a rabbit in heat. These are good rules for the seduction of a new partner, but they're also good rules for the "seduction" of someone you are already with. That is, your partner will appreciate this sort of approach, and quite likely be more forthcoming sexually.

It's not just the man who's at fault here, though. Both partners should make more of an effort to revive affection in the relationship. Spend more time kissing and hugging. When you arrive home in the evening, make a point of stopping for a hug and a kiss for a moment. Sit together on the couch in the evening with your arms around each other. Do the sorts of things you used to do early in your relationship: buy your partner flowers, call and talk on the phone during the day, say how much you love each other. A revival of romance will almost certainly lead to a revival of sex.

More Sex Please!

The most frequent sexual problem is one in which one partner wants more sex than the other, according to a recent survey by the American Association of Sex Educators, Counselors, and Therapists (AASECT). In most cases, it's the man who wants sex more often than the woman. This often causes real conflict. The man may feel that he has a right to have his needs satisfied. The woman feels that she shouldn't be forced to have sex when she doesn't want or need it. The man may begin to feel very resentful; after all, in our society there's usually an implicit contract between most partners, whether married or not, that monogamy is expected. Thus a man feels unfairly deprived of sex; he can't satisfy himself within the relationship, but he isn't supposed to go outside the relationship to have his needs satisfied. Of course men often *do* go outside the relationship for more sex, though that's opening Pandora's Box, and may result in the *end* of the relationship.

On the other hand women often complain that men are too insistent. It's not the frequency of sexual overtures, they may say, it's the manner in which the male makes those overtures. Women feel their men are too aggressive and insistent, that they expect an immediate response to any suggestion of sex. Men, however, would respond that they're doing nothing different from what they've always done; and it's often the case that while a woman is more sexually responsive early in a relationship—and thus more likely to respond to any and all sexual overtures—later in the relationship, often burdened by small children and added responsibilities, she becomes less so, and finds her mate's aggressive advances to be *too* aggressive and *too* insistent.

We've heard all sorts of comments from men about the problem of disparities of desire. One told us, "I would love to have sex with my wife any time, any place, and for any reason. She lets me have it once or twice a month. If she would even hand stroke me to orgasm it would help a lot, I would feel she still cares. She said I had enough sex during the first two years of marriage, and she has given me two children so that's all there is. I am constantly irritated and I'm afraid it's major gridlock." Other comments we've heard are "She begrudgingly gives a little," or quite simply "My wife refuses to have sex with me."

These are serious problems that threaten the very core of a relationship, and must be dealt with, not just to save your sex life, but to save your marriage or relationship. If what you just read seems to describe *your* relationship, you should talk about the issue. Find a quiet, relaxed time. Don't try to talk about it immediately after she has rejected a sexual advance, or with the idea that you'll be able to talk about it and then have sex. If necessary, schedule a time. If she says, "I don't want to talk about it now," ask her when would be a good time.

Tell her that you love her and want to keep the relationship happy, but that the frequency of sex has become a real problem for you. Ask her if she knows why she's no longer interested in sex. Suggest that she see a gynecologist if she feels there's a medical reason for her abstinence. Examine the following check list, and discuss each item together, to see if you can gain some insight into the problem. Some of the items in the list may quite clearly not be an issue, but others may lead you somewhere.

- Is she afraid of pregnancy?
- Does she act lovingly with you in nonsexual situations?
- Does she feel that the only time you want intimacy is when you want sex?
- Does she feel that the only time you ever really speak to her is when you want sex?
- Does she act uninterested, bored, or angry with you, or with something else?
- Is she constantly irritated with you for small annoyances?
- Is she worried about money matters?
- Does she feel that you don't help enough around the house?
- Is she constantly tired out from household chores?
- Are there problems with the in-laws on either side?
- Does she feel appreciated for her hard work, or does she feel taken for granted?
- Does she feel that you don't care about her sexual pleasure, and that you are not willing to help her find sexual satisfaction?
- Is she bored with the relationship?
- Does she seldom experience orgasm, and so has lost interest in sex?
- Is she getting back at you for something you've done?
- Does she feel too fat and out of condition to be attractive?
- Does she resent the fact that you've "let yourself go," and no longer finds you sexually attractive?

It's also possible that a hormonal imbalance or other medical problem may be causing the problem, so if she honestly can't think of any good reason for her lack of interest, it's a good idea for her to visit her doctor.

From this check list you can infer a number of solutions. If there are non-sexual problems that are spilling over into the sexual realm, those problems should be dealt with. Also, you should both agree not to use sex—rather, a *lack* of sex—as "punishment." That is a ploy that's likely to backfire, creating great resentment in the partner being punished. If there's a problem, deal with it directly—don't use sex as a weapon.

If the woman feels that the man rushes things too much, and is not loving enough in nonsexual ways, then he can easily remedy that. If she's feeling self-conscious about her figure, the man can reassure her that he still finds her attractive . . . and can join her in a diet and exercise program. (As you know by now, that alone will almost certainly increase her desire for sex.)

✠ ✠ Compromise! ✠ ✠

You can get all the incidental problems out of the way, and still come down to a basic incompatibility: One partner wants sex more often than the other. There may be no money or in-law problems, both partners may be very much in love, they may find each other physically attractive . . . and still one may want sex more often than the other. The only true remedy to such a problem is compromise. One partner will, in effect, reduce his or her expectations of sex, while the other partner will try harder to please more often.

For instance, take the case of John, one of the men in our study, a forty-six-year-old accountant. This was a case in which the *wife* wanted more sex than the husband. He was satisfied with sex a couple of times a week, but she wanted it every day. As a compromise, they still had intercourse twice a week, then, several days a week they made love but without intercourse. They would kiss and hug, and John would help his wife achieve an orgasm with a vibrator, his hand, or his mouth. John gave his wife the sexual attention she needed, and she didn't press him for daily intercourse.

✠ ✠ A Male Problem, Too ✠ ✠

It's not only the woman who loses desire for the man. There's a famous story about President Calvin Coolidge. He was visiting a research farm with the First Lady. He was taken on a tour in one direction, and the First Lady was taken in another direction. While visiting the chickens, Mrs. Coolidge was told how active the cocks were . . . how often they were capable of "servicing" a hen each day.

"Oh, interesting," she said. "See that the President hears that, would you?"

Later, when the President's party passed by, he was told that the First Lady made a point of saying he should be told about the cocks, and how often a cock could service a hen.

"Oh, same hen each time?" he asked.

"Oh, no sir, a different hen each time!"

"Ah, interesting . . . see that the First Lady hears that, would you."

It's an unfortunate truth that men lose sexual interest in their partners over time. In fact, this is not something peculiar to the human animal, but is common to the males of many other mammalian species. His post-orgasmic refractory period (the time after orgasm during which the penis relaxes), and the time between sexual episodes, increases. His interest in sex diminishes, and the time he dedicates to the sexual arousal of his partner diminishes, too!

Now, it's often said that such reduction in sexual interest is due to aging. However, we know this is not true, because when a man finds another sexual partner—a new partner or an extramarital liaison, for instance—his sexual stamina and interest suddenly increase again! In short, his penis keeps pace with his sexual interest.

I'm not suggesting that a man should find a new sexual partner in order to revive his sex life; he doesn't need to, as he can rebuild his sex life, increasing the level of sexual interest and time given over to arousal, using other methods. As you've already seen, exercise and improved diet will almost certainly improve desire. Bringing the spark of sexual excitement back into your sex lives will improve desire. And more attention to the woman's needs can help too. Her level of desire will improve, and the new energy in the sexual relationship will increase the man's desire. So that's what we'll look at next—what a woman wants and needs.

Sexual Position #2

Bringing variety into your sex life can help keep it alive—variety is the spice of sex. One way to add variety to your sex life is to make a point of trying different positions. They don't all have to bring intense sexual pleasure. Not all the positions you try *need to* provide intense sexual pleasure. Sometimes it's nice just to fool around a little, and see what happens. You may find a position that feels fantastic to both of you—or it may just make you laugh. That's okay, sex is all about fun.

Most of the modules in this book end with a suggested position. Why not try these positions as a way to bring variety into your sex life? We spoke in this module about the need to keep romance in your relationship, so how about trying this position? Side-by-side positions such as this can be very romantic; they are less strenuous than many positions, and they allow a couple to kiss and caress each other.

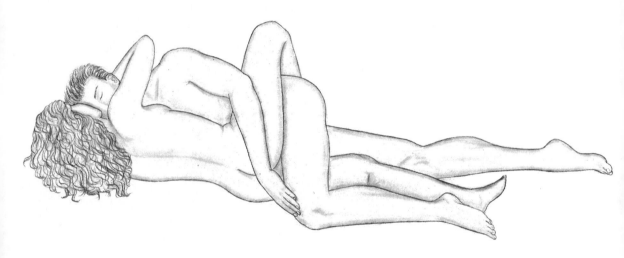

Module 5

What Turns On a Woman?

*I*f you ask a man what makes a man a great lover, you'll probably hear something like this: "Good looking, broad shoulders, muscular, large penis, gets it up when he wants, can thrust as long as he wants, and can come when and how often he wants." Almost a caricature of some kind of sex cyborg, really. Feminest Germaine Greer was right: "It is still assumed that a man should make love as if his principal intention was to people the wilderness."

Ask a woman what makes a man a great lover, and she'll tell you something *completely* different. You'll hear comments as far removed from our sex cyborg as Woody Allen is from Arnold Schwarzenegger. Here are a variety of women's comments taken from our study:

- "I must have a man who is friendly and kind. Without that I'm unable to relax and enjoy sex."
- "A man's age is not the object, what turns me on the most is if he has a boyish enthusiasm for my body and displays excitement."
- "He tells me how he feels about me, he doesn't rush me, and takes time to undress me slowly, all the while giving me compliments and kisses."
- "He arranges a comfortable, warm, safe, and romantic location for sex."
- "Once in bed we lie for ten or fifteen minutes, naked, simply holding each other, mouth to mouth. He takes adequate time to learn about my body and to explore the secret sensual areas."

- "I don't want an anxious, frantic, in-a-hurry man. I want one who has about the same sex drive as I, but is willing to wait a day or so if I'm not ready."
- "When he touches me with his hands, I want him to move tenderly around my face, neck, and shoulders. I guess tenderness is the essence."
- "He uses his fingertips lightly to skim over the surface of my skin and is responsive to my small sighs and moans and body movements. He uses his mouth slowly and kisses me everywhere. With his lips he sucks my flesh into his mouth and with the tip of his tongue stimulates my nerve endings."
- "During the whole process of lovemaking he talks to me, and I hear from him that he is utterly taken by me."
- "When he first moves inside me, he moves slowly and may even remain motionless for a time. It gives me time to feel his penis fill me up and I'm able to contract my vaginal muscles and close in snugly around his warm penis. Next, he makes slow careful thrusts and eventually quickens his depth and tempo to meet my counter thrusts. All the time he is verbalizing about his sensations. During intercourse he is frequently able to control his orgasm until I have had one or more. Or, when I need to be orally stimulated to orgasm or made to orgasm with his hand, he will oblige generously."
- "I like all aspects of sex. I like to have an orgasm in a variety of ways, and not always end up with intercourse as the major event."
- "Tenderness and loving patience brings on my best orgasm."
- "He does not put pressure on me to orgasm when I cannot."
- "When we have finished the active phase of our lovemaking he stays with me, and doesn't jump up or turn to sleep but continues kissing, touching, hugging, and providing the affection and attention I need most."
- "I want a man who satisfies my fantasy. If he is gentle and caring, that part of him becomes the fantasy."

According to the comments we found in this survey, women want a man who is loving, tender, and will demonstrate that the woman he is with is the only object of his affection. Women want to feel safe, and know that their men are excited by being with them. They need a man who will take his time—they don't want to be rushed—and will learn what pleases them. That's a far cry from the male idea of the sex machine.

They also want more nonsexual intimacy. When syndicated newspaper columnist Ann Landers asked her readership if they would be willing to swap sexual intercourse for more hugging and holding, she got around 100,000 responses . . . and an amazing 72,000 said "Yes!" they would give up intercourse if they got more holding! It's interesting to note that some studies show that about 72 percent of women say that they don't have orgasms during intercourse.

Is there a correlation here, perhaps? And if those 72,000 *were* having orgasms during intercourse, would they be more interested in intercourse?

Ideally a woman should have both holding and satisfying intercourse. However, this survey highlights the importance of nonsexual intimacy for women, something most men pay little attention to. For many inexperienced, anxious, immature, and selfish men, intimacy with their partner is all about sex, and sex is all about "a quick rub on the back, a kiss on each nipple, a finger in, and off he goes." Perhaps you've heard this joke:

> Question: What words of endearment do American men use during foreplay?
> Answer: "Hey, you awake?"

Perhaps if more men realized that nonsexual touching can easily turn into sexual touching, they'd be more interested in giving their partners the holding and gentle touching they need. While holding and hugging express love and caring that is not necessarily sexual, when two lovers are close, the pressing together of their bodies may start the reflex of sexual arousal.

⚜ ⚜ What Is She Looking For? ⚜ ⚜

What sort of man is she looking for? We've just heard how she wants to be treated in bed. But what would induce her to go to bed with a man? Again, from our surveys, this is what we found:

- "I need a warm, romantic, sympathetic man who is able to listen and respond interestingly to my conversation."
- "I like a man who is truly happy that I am a woman and cares for me as a woman and is able to accept my liberatedness or my *un*liberatedness."
- "I like a man who is natural. Not too systematic or mechanical, is not predictable or too-well rehearsed in his responses."
- "I love a man with a sense of humor, a bit of a tease, a man who smiles a lot and has nice teeth."
- "Women want every part of a man's body to smell good. Over that trim and tight stomach they would like him to be well dressed and healthy looking. No smokers please."
- "I like a man who is a natural, articulate, smooth, well-dressed gentleman with a little bit of spice, and who would not be afraid to give me a quick little pat on the ass, even if there was a chance we might be seen. He must be financially secure, but just because he has a little money he shouldn't expect that I'm going to fall all over him."
- "Passion and deep feelings and allowing me a glimpse of his weaknesses turns me on. I hope he cares about me and is passionate and lustful as hell."

- "Self-confidence, consideration; none of that macho shit. I like a man who displays a sense of ease, who is in control of his environment, and who is a polite but formidable adversary when other men are around."
- "I like a man who takes his time with me. He must not rush, or appear too anxious."
- "The most important qualities of a man, in or out of bed, are that he is honest, up front, and enthusiastic about me and our relationship. I don't want him to tell me stories, and I don't want him to make up flattering statements. I want to know he feels so strongly about me that regardless of any temptation of infidelity, he will not betray the relationship."
- "I need a man who is strong, who at times is willing to give me some of his strength, and make me the center of his universe."
- "If we're walking along the street he'll take my hand and on impulse may stop and abruptly give me a bold but warm kiss."

Well, maybe women *do* want superman! In any case, the male readers of this book may want to look over this list again, and see how they would match up. If they don't match closely, perhaps they can please their partners somewhat by trying to take on some of these characteristics. A sense of humor, self-confidence, a caring attentive attitude. There's not much to complain about here.

❧ ❧ A Woman's Arousal ❧ ❧

Arousal may be thought of as that part of sex that leads up to the actual sex act, and many women define arousal very broadly, at least as far as the average man is concerned. While a man thinks of arousal and foreplay as the same thing (and perhaps considers foreplay as too long if it goes over ten or fifteen minutes), many women consider the arousal stage as beginning hours before— ideally if not in practice.

Here are some of the things we were told at the Exercise Physiology Laboratory during these surveys. We asked women what they considered the most important "in bed" and "out-of-bed" forms of sexual arousal that were neglected by their mates. Here are the out-of-bed arousal activities that women wanted, listed with the most-mentioned first:

- Pleasant conversation, inquiring about her day, telling her you love her
- Looking into her eyes with interest
- Touching around her face
- Hugging, caressing, and light kissing
- Full-length body contact with heavy kissing
- Partially undressing her

Inquiring about her day! Pleasant conversation! Clearly men and women are on totally different wavelengths here. A man may raise the subject of sex while getting ready for bed, or even after getting into bed . . . several *hours* after the point at which he should have started getting his partner interested! A man wouldn't even consider the first two things on the list as sexual in any way, and the third is barely sexual. But that's what women say they want. Here's what we found they wanted during the in-bed arousal stage:

- More time touching nonvaginal areas
- Full body massage
- Kissing and nibbling around the neck and ears
- Kissing and licking the inner thighs, behind and on top of the knees and ankles
- Light and slow oral teasing and stimulation around and on the clitoris

More time touching nonvaginal areas? This is something most men will recognize; it's another version of the all-too-common complaint, "As soon as we get into bed the first thing he wants to do is dive down between my legs." Men want to get on with sex. Women want to spend more time leading up to it. The Elizabethan poet John Donne had the right idea, about 400 years ago:

> License my roving hands, and let them go
> Before, behind, between, above, below.

We also found that if men would just slow down a little, spend more time arousing their mates, they would get more out of sex. Ninety-four percent of the men in our study said that they enjoyed arousing their mate, and that when they did so they became more aroused themselves. Thirty percent said that it was the most important and intimate part of the sexual session. Furthermore, many men enjoy the control that extended foreplay gives them. They enjoy their partner's responses, both verbal and nonverbal, as they touch, kiss, caress, lick, and suck on various body parts . . . men find it to be a real turn-on to rouse their partners to greater levels of sexual excitement.

Ask a man what makes a great lover, and his answer is likely to include the word "penis" (or some euphemism for that organ) or refer to an erection or to intercourse. Such as, "A man who can keep it up," or "a man who can fuck several times in short succession." Ask a woman what makes a great lover, and she'll use words like "sensitive" and "caring," or say that she wants extra time hugging, kissing, and touching. In fact men and women regard the sex acts as different things. Women regard sex as warmth and intimacy, unhurried, sincere, regular touching, hugging, and kissing . . . outside bed as well as in. Men regard sex as . . . well, we all know what men regard as sex.

Here's a typical comment on this difference of perception, from one thirty-year-old woman: "In bed he always plays with my tits and thinks I'm being turned on . . . I'm not, and he won't believe me when I say 'if you really want to turn me on, rub my back and shoulders for a while. Then I'll be yours.'" Women often complain that men discontinue a particular sexual technique because they regard it as foreplay and are ready for the real thing—intercourse. Yet that technique could have brought on a wonderful orgasm while intercourse may not. Women regard sexual arousal as important as intercourse. They don't think of it as something to do to get ready for "real" sex, they think of it as good sex itself.

✖ ✖ So What Do Men Want? ✖ ✖

What do men want? Forget loving conversation, inquiries into how their day went . . . men are more basic animals. It's been said that what men most want is a "virgin who is a whore," and that's not far from the truth. It's also been said, by women all over the world, that "all men are dogs" (or pigs, or some other lower mammal). And again, it's not far from the truth. A man in heat shares many characteristics with a dog in heat. Understand this, ladies (as you probably already do), and you'll understand the man.

Ask men what they want during foreplay, and most (ninety-eight percent in our study) will suggest that their partners should touch, squeeze, and suck their penises more. Many (sixty-seven percent we found) also like to have their testicles handled. However, we also found that the average time the men in our study wanted to spend on arousal was thirty minutes. (Of course when they were thinking of arousal, they weren't thinking of pleasant conversation, or having their wives inquiring about their day!) On average, though, they only spent ten to fifteen minutes on arousal. Now, considering that most women say their men don't spend enough time on arousal, and that we found a fifteen- to twenty-minute "arousal deficit," it looks like there's plenty of room for improvement here. In fact this is something that can be negotiated fairly quickly! (Negotiation is always easy when both sides have a common goal.)

Another thing men commonly want is more oral sex, and more sexually aggressive women, too. That's not true for all men; some are still rather old-fashioned and believe that it's the woman's role to lie on her back and take whatever the man delivers—and not look like she's enjoying it too much, either. But many men complain that women don't make enough effort, that it's always left up to the man to initiate sex, and to do most of the work, too. Sometimes it's nice to be the passive partner, to have a mate who takes over and leads the sex play wherever she wants it to go.

While some men in our study already recognized the value of arousal—that their partners enjoyed it and that sex could be better for both partners—many men made comments that suggest that they have a lot to learn. Comments such as "Sex is intercourse, and all the rest is superfluous." "I don't especially care for too much foreplay, but she won't 'put out' without it!" And "Why can't women get their act together a little faster; rubbing on their clitoris all evening is not my idea of fun!" It's easy to get the impression that these men would heartily agree with humorist Don Herold's comment: "Women are not much, but they are the best other sex we have."

Unless these men reassess this attitude, and realize how counterproductive it is, they can kiss great sex good-bye. And they'll never be a great lover in their partner's eyes. The first step to becoming a good lover, though, is finding out what your mate really wants . . . which we'll do in Module 6.

Sexual Position #3

It's a good idea for the man to continue, during intercourse, the sort of caressing and kissing that his partner enjoys. Some positions work better than others for this. The plain old missionary position, for instance, rather limits the man's ability to caress and kiss his lover's body.

Try this position. It's a nice slow, relaxed position, in which the man can gently run his hands almost the complete length of his lover's body, caressing her legs, buttocks, hips, waist, breasts, and arms. He's also in a position to kiss her body and neck, and she can pull her leg up to allow him to slip his hand between her legs and touch her vaginal lips and clitoris.

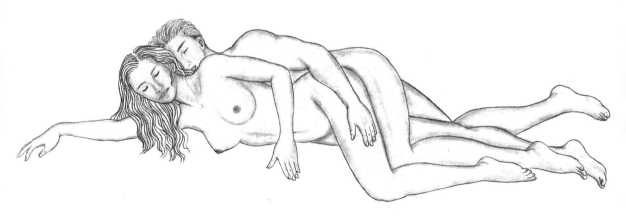

What Turns On a Woman?

Module 6

What Feels Good?

*I*t's almost a cliché that men don't know what women want. Of course it's often assumed that somehow women *do* know what men want, and that it's only men who are at fault here. In fact, while the gap between fantasy and reality may be greater for men, both sexes have got a lot to learn about what turns each other on.

✻ ✻ What Do You Want? ✻ ✻

Does you lover really know what you want from sex? Do *you* really know what you want? Are you quite sure you know what your lover enjoys? It's easy to blame our partners when we're not getting what we want, but first stop and consider how often you *talk* about sex. Most couples get physical right away, and find out by trial and error what "works." This is natural considering the type of courting common in Western societies. We don't like to broach the subject of sex with a new partner for fear of rejection. Instead we use physical communication to move toward lovemaking—gentle, nonsexual touches, followed by kissing, followed by more sexually oriented touching, and so on. Actual *talk* may not occur (until, perhaps, a breathless request to move to the bedroom—or until it's all over).

There are other reasons for not talking about sex. Many men feel that asking what their lover wants betrays sexual naiveté—that they should know what good sex is without having to ask. Many women feel it's just not nice to talk about sex, even with the man with whom they share a bed. He should know what works without having to be told, anyway.

But trial and error is an inefficient learning method. Even the most experienced lover can be lacking in some areas, as everyone's sexual desires are different. Your partner may have had previous partners with completely different sexual tastes. What you have found pleased other lovers may turn off your current partner. How can your lover really know what you want, unless you tell him or her? For instance, contrary to popular opinion, some women do not particularly enjoy breast stimulation. Some even find it uncomfortable. How is a man to know that, unless he's told? After all, most women *do* enjoy breast stimulation. How can a man know what type of woman he's got his hands on (literally)?

If you are early in your relationship, here's a tip that will pay dividends in the long term; start talking about sex right now. Talk with your partner about what he or she enjoys, and tell your partner what turns *you* on now. It's actually much easier to begin talking early in a relationship than later. Wait until later and habits have already been created, sexual ruts have become traps, and it's even become a habit to not talk about sex. Breaking habits can be difficult. If you talk about sex early on, and get into the habit of talking about it regularly, you'll be glad you did later.

So, whether you are in a new or old relationship, here's an idea for you. Plan a romantic evening, with flowers, candlelight, soft music . . . and the following questionnaire. Make copies of the questionnaire, then fill them in separately. You may find some of the questions difficult to answer. You may feel that an honest answer about your compatibility could hurt your partner. So agree beforehand that you will both be sincere, with the understanding that both of you are interested in improving your relationship, not creating conflict. In fact, you'll probably find this little process a lot of fun. Discussing your answers will likely be a turn-on for both of you.

Feel free to make notes on the questionnaire. For instance, one of the questions asks if you would like more caressing during foreplay. You may want to note what type of caressing you particularly enjoy.

1. How would you rate sexual compatibility with your partner?

❑ Very compatible—couldn't be better
❑ Compatible—quite good, but room for improvement
❑ Fair—it's okay, but there's work to be done
❑ Not compatible—we've got some problems to deal with

2. How do you think your partner would rate your compatibility?

- ❑ Very compatible—couldn't be better
- ❑ Compatible—quite good, but room for improvement
- ❑ Fair—it's okay, but there's work to be done
- ❑ Not compatible—we've got some problems to deal with
- ❑ I don't know

3. How well do you talk with your partner about sex?

- ❑ Very well—we talk a lot
- ❑ Well—we talk now and again, but it could be better
- ❑ Not too well—we rarely talk
- ❑ Badly—we almost never talk

4. How do you think your partner will respond to Question 3?

- ❑ Very well—we talk a lot
- ❑ Well—we talk now and again, but it could be better
- ❑ Not too well—we rarely talk
- ❑ Badly—we almost never talk
- ❑ I don't know

5. How would you describe the trust you feel for your partner? How confident are you of your partner's love and loyalty?

- ❑ Excellent—I trust my partner implicitly
- ❑ Quite good—I trust my partner most of the time
- ❑ Not too good—I wish I could trust my partner more
- ❑ Not at all—I don't trust my partner in any way!

6. How do you think your partner will respond to Question 5?

- ❑ Excellent—I trust my partner implicitly
- ❑ Quite good—I trust my partner most of the time
- ❑ Not too good—I wish I could trust my partner more
- ❑ Not at all—I don't trust my partner in any way!
- ❑ I don't know

7. How would you describe the intimacy you give your partner during *non*sexual activities—touching, holding hands, kissing, etc.?

- ❑ Great—we're like new lovers
- ❑ Good—we are quite affectionate
- ❑ Okay—but it could be better
- ❑ Lousy—we're more like friends than lovers

8. How do you think your partner would describe the intimacy you provide during *non*sexual activities?

❑ Great—we're like new lovers
❑ Good—we are quite affectionate
❑ Okay—but it could be better
❑ Lousy—we're more like friends than lovers
❑ I don't know

9. How would you describe the intimacy you give your partner during sex?

❑ Great—we're like new lovers
❑ Good—we are quite affectionate
❑ Okay—but it could be better
❑ Lousy—it's just sex, not lovemaking

10. How do you think your partner would describe the intimacy you give during sex?

❑ Great—we're like new lovers
❑ Good—we are quite affectionate
❑ Okay—but it could be better
❑ Lousy—it's just sex, not lovemaking
❑ I don't know

11. Generally your sex life is . . . ?

❑ Fantastic—it's hard to imagine it getting better
❑ Good—it's quite good, though there's room for improvement
❑ Fair—it's okay, but there's *lots* of room for improvement
❑ Bad—we don't enjoy a sharing sexual relationship

12. How do you think your partner will respond to question 11?

❑ Fantastic—it's hard to imagine it getting better
❑ Good—it's quite good, though there's room for improvement
❑ Fair—it's okay, but there's *lots* of room for improvement
❑ Bad—we don't enjoy a sharing sexual relationship
❑ I don't know

13. How many minutes of foreplay do you normally have?

_____ minutes

14. How many minutes of foreplay would you prefer?

_____ minutes

15. Which activities do you use during foreplay, which would you like to use more often, and which do you think your partner would like to use more often?

	We use	I'd like to use more often	I think my partner would like to use more often
Sexual talk	❏	❏	❏
Pornography (video, magazines, books, etc.)	❏	❏	❏
Hugging	❏	❏	❏
Kissing	❏	❏	❏
Deep kissing	❏	❏	❏
Massaging	❏	❏	❏
Caressing	❏	❏	❏
Hand stimulation	❏	❏	❏
Gentle biting	❏	❏	❏
Nipple stimulation (woman)	❏	❏	❏
Nipple stimulation (man)	❏	❏	❏
Oral sex	❏	❏	❏
Rectal stimulation	❏	❏	❏
Vibrator stimulation	❏	❏	❏
Other mechanical devices (_____)	❏	❏	❏
Other _____	❏	❏	❏
Other _____	❏	❏	❏
Other _____	❏	❏	❏

16. What sexual activity (or combination of activities) normally leads to orgasm for you, and which of these activities would you like to use more often?

	We use	I'd like to use more often
Intercourse	❏	❏
Hand stimulation	❏	❏
Oral sex	❏	❏
Vibrator stimulation	❏	❏
Other mechanical devices	❏	❏
Rectal stimulation	❏	❏
Other _____	❏	❏

17. Is there activity you especially like that enhances orgasm, or one that you would like to use to enhance orgasm?

- ❏ Sexual talk
- ❏ Pornography
- ❏ Hugging
- ❏ Kissing
- ❏ Deep kissing
- ❏ Massaging
- ❏ Caressing
- ❏ Hand stimulation
- ❏ Gentle biting
- ❏ Nipple stimulation
- ❏ Oral sex
- ❏ Vibrator stimulation
- ❏ Other mechanical devices
- ❏ Rectal stimulation
- ❏ Testicular stimulation
- ❏ Hair pulling, scratching, or biting
- ❏ Other _____
- ❏ Other _____
- ❏ Other _____

When you finish the questionnaires, get together and compare them. If you have anything but great communication with your partner you'll probably be surprised by some of the answers, and almost certainly find ways in which you can improve your enjoyment of sex. You'll probably even find that some of the things your partner would like you to do for him or her you would enjoy also. (You may also find yourself feeling sexually aroused before you've finished reviewing all the answers. That's okay!) Good sex is a win/win situation.

It's important to be accepting, sensitive, and tolerant of your partner's responses—don't belittle his or her feelings or wishes. For instance, it's common for men to believe they provide enough intimacy and communication, while women commonly complain that their partners do *not*. Clearly there's a perception gap here, and if one partner *believes* there's a problem then there is. Discuss what you can do to improve the situation; don't just dismiss the issue out of hand. Don't feel threatened or hurt. If your partner's response is not what you expected, be grateful for the opportunity to correct the problem, not angry. And be careful not to interrupt your partner—let your partner finish what he or she has to say before responding.

You need not discuss—or insist on discussing—past sexual exploits with your partner. The purpose of this questionnaire is not confession of past sins; it's not a "confession will cleanse your soul" sort of thing. On the other hand, things may come out of these questions and your discussions that you weren't expecting. Remember, though, the more accepting you are of any unexpected information the greater will be your future trust and the strength of your relationship. The more specific you are about your desires, the more responsive your partner is likely to be. Recognize that sex is a very strange thing; you can't expect it to be logical. People find sexual pleasure in the most unlikely ways, but there's nothing wrong with that. The author W. Somerset Maugham once said, "There is hardly anyone whose sexual life, if it were broadcast, would not fill the world at large with surprise and horror." It's a shame that knowledge of someone's desires should induce "horror," and it doesn't have to be that way . . . but what's important in his comment is the recognition that sex covers such a variety of behaviors that there really is no norm. Try to accept your partner's pleasures as simply part of the rich tapestry of sexual life, no stranger or more unacceptable than other sexual tastes. Like the British judge who said, "I have long lost any capacity for surprise where sex is concerned," understand that everyone's sexual desires are different, and what surprises you may seem quite normal to many other people.

Some of the questions will lead to more specific answers and solutions than others. If you find that you have a problem with nonsexual intimacy and communication, you should discuss what you can do to improve things—you might make an effort to be more affectionate to your partner in nonsexual situations, and be more careful in listening to your partner when he or she talks to you. On the other hand, if your partner wants more oral sex, that's easily remedied!

After you've talked about your responses, what better time to begin rectifying the problems than right now? As you make love, bear in mind responses to the questions about what your partner enjoys during sex, and what might be improved. If each of you is attentive to the other's needs and wishes, you will have the best sex of your life.

Sexual Position #4

The position shown on the following page is sometimes known as the *Scissors*. The man is on top with one leg between the woman's thighs and one leg over her hip. It's usually easier for the man to enter the woman while in the "missionary position," and then move into this position. The man may support himself on his shoulder, or even move around until the partners' bodies make a cross, resting his body on both elbows. The position is quite comfortable for prolonged intercourse—though the man should be careful that his penis doesn't slip out of his partner and poke her during vigorous thrusting!

This is a great position for the woman to caress the man's buttocks and play with his testicles and rectum. She can also stimulate the man's prostate (see Module 30) by pressing on the area between his rectum and testicles— and use the scrotal tug (described in Module 11) to slow down his ejaculation. For this reason it's a good idea for the man to lie with his head on the woman's left side, so she can reach him with her right hand, assuming she is right-handed. If she is left-handed shift sides, so his head is at her right side, leaving her left hand free.

The man may wish to caress the woman's breasts, although it's also a wonderful position for the man to simply absorb himself in his own pleasure, concentrating on the feeling of his penis inside his partner and the manual stimulation she provides.

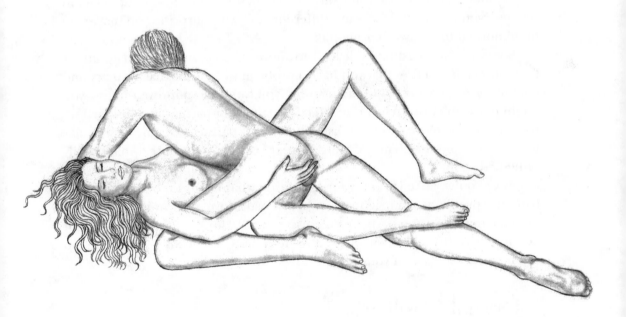

Module 7

Anatomy 101——The Penis

For something that gives so much pleasure, the penis seems to provoke an awful lot of distress. Sometimes it simply doesn't work properly—it doesn't get hard, or if it does get hard it finishes its job way too soon. But even when it *does* work properly, its a source of worry for many men: Is it big enough? Is it well shaped? Too thin? Is it bent to one side?

Here are a few words of comfort. Most penises are nowhere near as big as their owners would like, very few penises are in the superlarge category, they all look pretty odd . . . and most women don't really care about their partner's penis size or shape!

Of course *size* is the major concern for many men. Is my penis smaller than other men's? Will a woman think it's too small? Will she enjoy sex with my penis? Well, most penises are really not so big, anyway. The average Caucasian male has a penis that is 6.2 inches in length when erect. Folklore is right about black men's penises being larger—but only marginally. The average black man has a penis that is 6.4 inches when erect. (Get a ruler and take a look at how long two-tenths of an inch is; nothing dramatic.) Strangely, though, white men tend to think their penises are smaller than they actually are (they estimate the length at slightly under 6 inches on average) while black men tend to think their penises are slightly larger (6.7 inches on average).

And what do women think? Most want a man who knows what to do with his penis rather than a man with a big one. They want a lover who is considerate, who takes his time, who keeps an erection for a reasonable period of time, who doesn't prematurely ejaculate (see Module 11), and who doesn't withdraw as soon as he's "finished." However, most women describe their "fantasy" penis as being "very large." (Perhaps the ideal is not just a man who knows how to use his penis, but a man who knows how to use his *large* penis!) Aside from fantasy, though, many women say that intercourse with a large penis—over seven inches, say—is painful, as it drives against the cervix.

The fact is, most women are quite satisfied with the average-sized penis, whatever they may fantasize about. No doubt you've seen or heard divorce statistics on the TV or in magazines. You know the kind . . . this percentage of marriages breaks down for financial reasons. This percentage because one partner wants more sex than the other, and so on. But how often have you seen a "penis too small" category?

❧ ❧ Can You Make It Bigger? ❧ ❧

No, at least not without a surgical implant. (And do you *really* want someone cutting your penis?) The length and diameter of the penis appear to be genetically determined. The penis has three chambers of spongy tissue that fill with blood during an erection. Once you've finished puberty, these chambers are fixed in size. Sorry.

Cheer up, you don't need to make it bigger anyway. Our perceptions of the penis are warped by fantasy. Mankind worships the penis; the phallic symbol has been with us for millennia. These days we may not put statues of huge penises in our temples, but we worship the penis in other ways. *Playgirl* Magazine shows pictures of well-endowed men with semierect penises, while the letters in men's magazines commonly refer to 8-, 9-, and 10-inch penises as if they were the norm. Reality is very different—only one man in 10,000 has a penis that is 9 inches or longer. (The Kinsey study found that almost all men who claimed to have 10-inch penises actually had 8-inch penises.)

Ask a man what he first notices about a woman, and he may start with her face, but next he'll mention her breasts and butt. (In many cases her face comes third!) Women look at men in a different way, though. True, they often mention "nice tight buns." But they also talk about his eyes, hair, smile, and nonphysical attributes such as sense of humor and a friendly, affectionate attitude. They rarely mention "the bulge between his legs."

You'll often hear that sex is all in the mind, and penis size is a great example of this. Men with slightly smaller than average penises often underestimate the size, and feel insecure in their intimate relationships, while men with average and above average penises tend to *greatly* overestimate the size. One man is unhappy, the other satisfied. But the truth is that there often isn't much difference between the two. And the man with the smaller penis may well be the better lover.

✻ ✻ So How Big Is It? ✻ ✻

Okay, so you really have to know how you compare. For what it's worth, here's how. Measure your penis along the topside, from the pubic bone—the point at which the penis attaches to your body—to the tip of the penis. And measure the circumference around the widest point of the penis. Depending on what you push or pull, you can get many different measurements. Erection size can vary from day to day, too.

✻ ✻ When flaccid, how long is your penis? ✻ ✻

The nonerect penis generally ranges between 1.5 and 6 inches, with an average of 4.3 inches for black men and 3.8 inches for white men. However, the size of the flaccid penis varies tremendously from hour to hour. In the middle of the night it often shrinks so far it looks like it's trying to climb back inside! (In any case, who cares how big it is when it's resting?)

✻ ✻ When nonerect, what is the circumference of your penis? ✻ ✻

The flaccid penis ranges from around 1.75 to 5.25 inches, with an average of 3.8 inches for both black and Caucasian men. Again, your results may vary with the time of day.

✻ ✻ When erect, how long is your penis? ✻ ✻

Erect penises generally range from 2.75 to 9 inches.

✻ ✻ When erect, what is the circumference of your penis? ✻ ✻

The circumference of the erect penis ranges from around 3.5 inches to 6.5, with an average of 4.8.

We can think of a few results of this little measuring session. You may have discovered that you are larger than you thought. You may have found that you are nowhere near as large as you originally thought, that you are only average or slightly above. Even if you've discovered that you are smaller than most men, there's no need to be upset. There's nothing you can do to change the size (excepting surgery), but you *can* concentrate on other areas of your sexual persona, to become a better lover in ways that really matter. (And those of you who discovered that you are larger than most men, don't get smug. Remember, it's not how big it is, it's how well you use it!)

✸ ✸ You're Still Concerned? ✸ ✸

If you are still concerned about the size of your penis, if you still worry that it's too small, talk with your partner. You'll find that it's less of a concern to her than to you. You might try the following little experiment, too.

Set aside some time to play "doctor" with your mate. Find a comfortable environment—make a fire in the fireplace and set some warm, soft blankets on the floor in front of the fire, for instance. Turn the lights down a little; you want soft lighting, not a bright glare.

Now, the two of you can observe your genital areas. Use a mirror so you can both get a better view. Let your partner tell you what your penis looks like. Don't worry if she doesn't use a reverent tone when talking about your penis; they are, after all, strange-looking things! Encourage her to caress and kiss your penis, and you can both watch as it grows. It's really a remarkable process, one that we usually ignore in the rush toward sex. Reciprocate, too; gently touch and stroke between her legs, and tell her how her vagina and clitoris appear to you. Many women think of their genitals as quite ugly, and are often surprised that men can find them attractive.

Touching, examining, and talking about your body in this way helps to alleviate your concerns, and allows you to realize that your partner can fully appreciate your penis even if you're not built like an Egyptian obelisk! It can get you quite aroused, too, which is always nice.

Sexual Position #5

Okay, students, listen up. Tonight's position is one in which the vagina is constricted around the penis, which seems apt in this module—if the man's penis *is* a little small, this provides a nice tight fit. And if it's not small, he'll still find the feeling of tightness very pleasurable.

The woman lies on her back, with her legs drawn up, her thighs on her stomach. (This position is referred to as the *crab's position* in the Kama Sutra, as the woman's legs appear as a crab's claws retracted.)

The man kneels before the woman, with his knees on either side of her. After entering the woman, the man can hold onto the woman's legs, pulling them back to his chest, to help maintain balance.

Anatomy 102—The Clitoris

*I*n this module we are going to take a close look at the clitoris, and learn what it does and how to *use* it.

The clitoris is the female equivalent of the penis. It's almost the same appendage—in every fetus a mass of tissue will develop into a clitoris or penis, depending on the sex chromosomes that the fetus inherits from its parents.

Unlike the penis, though, the clitoris is hidden away—it's quite possible for a man to live his married life, to father many children, without ever seeing the clitoris or knowing of its existence (as undoubtedly many men have done in sexually repressive or prudish cultures). The most sensitive of areas on most women, the clitoris is tucked away under a hood of skin, hidden by the lips of the labia, above the vaginal opening. In order to expose the clitoris the labial lips must be parted, as shown in the picture on the following page.

Once it's exposed you can see that the clitoris looks like a minipenis. It's a shaft, usually about an inch long, though sometimes much longer or shorter. It has a head (the glans) and a foreskin. And during arousal it becomes engorged with blood, as does the penis—it gets wider and, perhaps, longer, though at the height of arousal it may shrink below its hood, and almost disappear entirely in some cases.

There's an important manner in which the clitoris differs from all other sexual organs—it's the only organ that appears to have no purpose but to provide pleasure. Which is proof, some say, that God wants women to have good

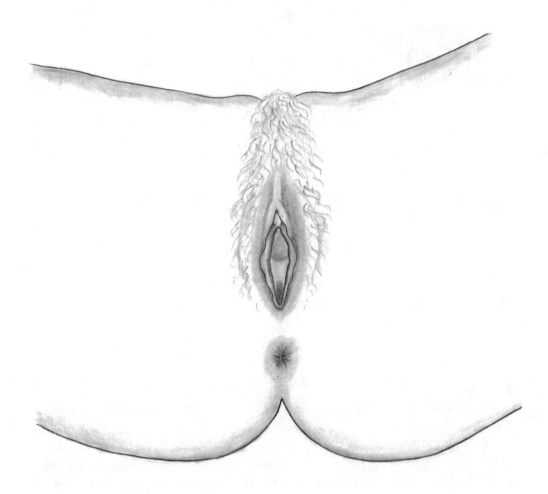

sex. And that brings us to the great "clitoral versus vaginal orgasm" debate. Dr. Sigmund Freud believed—and, unfortunately, managed to convince a whole generation—that clitoral sex was "immature," and that mature women got sexual pleasure from vaginal sex alone.

Modern research shows that nothing's black and white—you can't use sweeping generalizations to describe every woman's sexuality. Most women, it seems, require some sort of clitoral stimulation to reach orgasm (as reported by as many as 70 percent of women in some studies), while many other women report that clitoral stimulation is *not* required (which isn't to say that it's not desired, of course). Some women can reach orgasm from vaginal sex alone, and some even from nipple stimulation. Studies show that 30 percent to 40 percent of women routinely orgasm during intercourse. Everyone's different.

How, then, to stimulate the clitoris? For some reason the clitoris is placed so that it is not directly stimulated during sexual intercourse (proof, some might say, that God also wanted women to enjoy masturbation and oral sex). Clitoral stimulation during intercourse is possible, but you must make an effort, because it may not happen automatically. Even in the "missionary" position (with the woman on her back and the man on top), the clitoris will probably not be stimulated, unless the man "rides high," moving his body forward so that his pubic bone rubs against the clitoris. Or the man may penetrate deeply and then churn around, moving his pelvis from side to side in a circular motion. But for most couples this doesn't work well.

The clitoris really needs direct stimulation—manual or oral stimulation, or even stimulation by some kind of sex toy (which we'll discuss in Modules 16 and 17). In some positions the clitoris may be touched during intercourse (by the man or woman), providing the woman with both clitoral and vaginal stimulation. Or the clitoris alone may be stimulated, as a prelude to intercourse or as an end in itself.

The following is an exercise in clitoral stimulation in which the man will work toward giving his lover an orgasm through clitoral stimulation. The idea is not just to arouse her before intercourse, but to bring her to orgasm without intercourse. Intercourse following is fine, of course, but make sure she orgasms first. We said "work toward," though, because in some cases she may not quite get to orgasm. That's okay, practice makes perfect—try again.

1. Begin with a twenty-minute oil massage (I'll discuss massage more in Modules 12 and 13). Then, with both of you lying down facing each other, in bed or on another comfortable surface, spend ten or fifteen minutes simply kissing and caressing each other. The man's leg can be between the woman's legs, with his thigh pressing and slowly moving against the woman's pubic area.

2. Next, the man should kneel next to the woman, facing her. He should spend several minutes gently stroking her pubic hair rhythmically with both hands.

3. With one hand the man will gently separate the lips that cover her vagina—she may be damp by now, but if not he can lick a finger to lubricate it, or lubricate the vagina directly by licking up and down the lips, separating them with his tongue.

4. The man will then softly stroke in a circular motion around her clitoris, using a finger or thumb. The large flat area of the thumb is excellent for this—perhaps that's what it was designed for. Don't be rough, and make sure the clitoral area is lubricated with fluid from the vagina or saliva—how it is applied is up to you. As you stroke you may need to periodically relubricate the area.

5. As the man strokes, she may enjoy being kissed on other parts of the body. She may also want to touch and caress her own breasts and nipples while

he plays with her clitoris.

6. As she becomes more aroused, she may want stronger pressure and a faster circular motion on the clitoris. It's very difficult for a man to know how much pressure and speed is needed, so the woman ought to tell him exactly how to proceed. But she shouldn't forget to tell him when he's got it just right. Positive reinforcement, as all educators know, is a powerful learning tool. She should also let him know if she needs more lubrication.

7. Looking closely at the clitoris you'll notice the pink head appear and disappear inside its clitoral hood as the thumb or finger makes its rounds. The man should try *very gently* rolling the clitoral head between his thumb and index finger or middle finger.

8. Now, with his other hand, the man can insert one or more fingers into her vagina. Make sure the lips and vaginal wall are well lubricated, and insert the fingers gently and slowly, all the while maintaining stimulation on the clitoris.

9. The man can further stimulate the clitoris by gently sucking on it, or by licking around the clitoris in the same way he rubbed around with his finger or thumb.

10. The man will continue arousing her, following her instructions and watching for nonverbal gestures that indicate when all is going well, or when he should adjust the pressure and motion. If things *are* going well, by this time she may find giving verbal instructions difficult, so nonverbal cues may be all he has to work with.

11. As her sexual arousal continues, the woman may want stronger, more rapid pressure on the clitoris. The man needs patience. He shouldn't rush things and give up too early so he can get to intercourse. Take things slowly. In the case of a *pre-orgasmic* woman (that is, a woman who has not yet learned how to have an orgasm) this technique may not cause an orgasm the first few times, but just try again (and see Module 9 for more information on techniques to help women who have trouble reaching orgasm). Like everything else, good sex takes practice. Luckily, practice is fun.

Sexual Position #6

Here's an interesting position shown on the following page in which you can continue the clitoral stimulation. Admittedly there's a fairly limited range of motion for the man's pelvic region, but he can reach around with his hand and stroke his partner's clitoris, while moving his penis in and out with a gentle rocking motion. The woman can help with the rocking, too, by pushing against the floor with her feet.

Module 9

From Pre-Orgasm to Orgasm

*M*en are very penis-oriented. Given the option many men would go directly to intercourse without worrying about arousal or foreplay. In fact, a common statement from men is "I wish she would come while we are having intercourse." Men want intercourse, they want their partners to enjoy it and they want both partners to orgasm during intercourse.

Well, women *do* enjoy intercourse, but not in the same way that men do. Most women don't climax through intercourse, so it's a good idea for men to find other ways to help their partners reach orgasm. That's what we'll look at in this module. We'll also discuss a very common sexual problem, what has come to be known as *pre-orgasm*.

✄ ✄ The Pre-Orgasmic Woman ✄ ✄

Many women are what's known these days as *pre-orgasmic*. This simply means that they have not found out how to have an orgasm. In the past a much uglier, guilt-provoking term—*frigid*—was used, but the term pre-orgasmic is a more optimistic one. It recognizes that all women are biologically capable of having an orgasm. It's just that some haven't yet done so.

Incidentally, pre-orgasmic women keep their secret well—their men often have no idea they have a pre-orgasmic mate. These women have become very accomplished at faking it, as was demonstrated in the movie *When Harry Met Sally* fake-orgasm scene. As Fanny Brice once said, "Men always fall for frigid women because they put on the best show." Faking orgasm is not such a great idea, though. It's dishonest, and can hurt both partners. The woman feels inadequate and a failure. And if she tells her partner that she's been faking it, he's likely to feel inadequate . . . why does she need to fake it, is he not good enough? Both may be inclined to avoid sex because the outcome has always been failure.

Unfortunately, many pre-orgasmic women have problems because they believe sex is dirty, not something nice girls do. In this day and age it may seem strange that such Victorian attitudes persist, but persist they do. Women often learn that sex is something that men want and women have to give to keep them happy. That it's wrong for a woman to initiate sexual activity or take an active role, and that any sexual excitement or enjoyment on her part is something to be embarrassed about, not enjoyed.

There are other reasons for an inability to respond sexually, of course. She may have been sexually abused as a child. She may have been raped—many rape victims suffer from a lack of sexual desire and responsiveness. Or her partner may have been an insensitive clod! Whatever the reason, though, if a woman has a partner who is patient and willing to spend time talking about the problem—and helping her take steps to deal with it—she's got a very good chance of learning how to allow herself to orgasm.

Pre-orgasmic women have a lot of help available to them these days. There are many sex therapists and even "pre-orgasmic" clinics at hospitals. A pre-orgasmic woman can attend these clinics to learn about her genitals, and perhaps become orgasmic through masturbation techniques taught at the clinics. She may even discover techniques that allow her to achieve orgasm with her partner during sexual intercourse.

❧ ❧ Sensate Focusing for the Pre-Orgasmic Woman ❧ ❧

A tool commonly used to teach pre-orgasmic women to reach orgasm—and to help men who have problems maintaining erections during intercourse—is known as *sensate focusing*. This is a method that builds sexual self-awareness, confidence and mutual trust between sexual partners.

Talk together about orgasm, and what the female partner feels would be necessary for her to have regular orgasms. She should explore her body alone, especially her clitoris, and focus on any pleasurable sensations she finds, and the sort of touch that brings them about. She should try to have an orgasm while alone, and pay special attention to exactly how she achieves this orgasm. Eventually the aim is to achieve orgasm with her partner participating, of course, but it's helpful for the woman to experience it alone, too.

Later you can begin sensate-focusing sessions. The Masters and Johnson program of sensate focusing is an extended program that moves very slowly, beginning with learning to touch each other's face and the nonsexual parts of each other's body. Here's an abbreviated program of sensate focusing, concentrating on sexual touch.

The female lies on her back. Her mate lies beside her and places his hand on top of her hand so that his fingers are interlaced with hers or are directly on top of her fingers—or she may try placing his hand *beneath* hers. With the former method his hand follows hers, in the latter case her hand moves his. She lightly caresses her sensitive areas and he makes mental notes of the force and speed of her movements, and watches nonverbal indications of her pleasure. This procedure should be practiced several times and she should orgasm whenever she can.

When the man feels he knows how to give his mate the sexual pleasure she's able to give herself, he can take over and caress her directly, without her assistance. She can try to heighten the feeling by using sexual fantasies during the sex play—she can close her eyes, lie back, and enjoy the caressing while imagining whatever excites her.

The woman can direct his stroking with simple statements: "I like that," "I don't like that," "Please move to a different area for now," or "Please, put your hand on top of my hand for a while." In the last case the woman takes over, relieving the man of having to know exactly what is expected of him, and lets him follow her motions again.

It's important to remember that the man cannot assume responsibility for the woman's orgasms. He can assist her with his hand, fingers, mouth or penis, but that's about all—unless he's a magician. He can learn the necessary techniques, but ultimately the orgasm is hers. She has to allow herself the pleasure of an orgasm, so if she is holding back completely the man should not feel that he is somehow responsible for the failure.

If the woman cannot orgasm with the above methods, you may want to try clitoral stimulation with a vibrator (see Module 16) using a slow speed to reduce the intensity. She can use it alone the first time. It's not an act of "unfaithfulness." The intention is not to let the vibrator replace closeness, and not to use it so frequently that she becomes dependent upon it for her orgasms (repeated use may desensitize the clitoris), but it's one way to heighten pleasure and make it easier to achieve orgasm when she is first "learning."

As the two of you proceed, try to experience female orgasm with the aid of the hand or the man's mouth, during finger play, during intercourse, and occasionally with your vibrator. Or use any method you happen to come up with.

Here's the perfect use of the sensate focusing. This is a technique used by a fifty-year-old man in our study to stimulate his partner to orgasm. The intention of this module is to focus on the woman achieving her orgasm *before* intercourse. Sure, go on and finish your session any way you wish, but try the following technique first, as described by the fifty-year-old:

1. We start our arousal early, in a romantic vein. We begin with an intimate dinner, for instance. We talk, kiss, touch each other. Nothing sexual, just tender and loving.

2. At home, during foreplay, I place my hand beneath my lover's, so she can direct my attention and touching to different parts of her body, and to dictate the pace and type of caress.

3. She directs my hands over her nipples, stomach, down her legs, and inside the thighs. When she gets to the vaginal area, I put my hand on top of hers so that I can feel her manipulate the lips and clitoris.

4. I then place her hand atop mine again, and continue stimulating the clitoris in the way she's just shown me. She guides my fingers to the right spot at the correct time.

5. As I circle her clitoris with my thumb or middle finger, she exerts the exact amount of pressure and directs my movement for maximum stimulation to her clitoris.

6. With her hand on mine she can move away from the clitoris if she wishes or intensify the pressure and speed of orgasm.

7. If she wants oral sex, I place her hand on her clitoris and with my tongue follow the movements and pace that she dictates.

8. I make my free hand available for her to place on any other part of the body.

9. Using my finger on her clitoris I occasionally dip down between her lips and sample the wetness or sneak a finger into her vagina and bring the moisture up to lubricate the clitoris.

10. We continue like this until she has reached orgasm. Then I take my turn. Often I use the same technique of placing my lover's hands over mine, in order to direct her for my maximum pleasure.

Sexual Position #7

A position that allows clitoral stimulation seems appropriate here. Most women are unable to orgasm during intercourse, so they need extra help.

Clitoral stimulation during intercourse can provide that help. And the *oceanic* position is a great way to provide that stimulation.

The oceanic position is named for the Polynesian islanders who used it so much . . . and so upset the Christian missionaries who believed the only sexual position acceptable was the simple man-on-top position that came to be known as the *missionary* position.

You won't be struck down by lightning if you use this position, except perhaps the sexual lightning that occurs when everything works just right. This position is wonderful for ejaculatory control, and for helping the woman to orgasm during intercourse.

The man's not going to do much vigorous thrusting in this position! He can put his penis into her vagina, but not very deeply; he can use one hand to

move the penis, almost as if he's using his penis as a dildo to excite her labia and clitoris. He can use the other hand to gently rub her clitoris. This is a good starting position, one in which the woman may get very aroused before he moves to a position that allows full penetration.

With practice a fit couple can take this position further. They may move into the position we've shown in Module 17, with both the man and woman sitting up higher, the woman supporting herself on her hands. They may also be able to use a position in which the man is kneeling completely upright, holding his partner up so both are face to face (like the standing position in Module 25). Even if you are not both in the best condition, you'll probably find it fairly easy to move into a position in which he is kneeling, sitting on his thighs, while she is sitting on top of him, with her arms around him.

By the way, you should also try the "ultimate" position that we've shown at the end of Module 11. This position provides a wonderful way to experience extended intercourse—the man can control his orgasm and provide manual stimulation for the woman, too.

Module 10

Extending Pre-Orgasm and Orgasm

Sexual sensation is often described as comprising four phases: arousal, pre-orgasmic sensation, orgasm, and post-orgasmic sensation. In this module we're going to take a look at how to extend the most sensitive of phases, the pre-orgasmic and orgasmic sensations, the phases immediately before and during orgasm. The first is a state of highly aroused pleasure—you are not simply getting worked up to orgasm, but you are almost there. Just a little more stimulation and over you go, across the boundary to orgasm. The second, of course, is the height of sexual pleasure, the point at which we completely lose control to our sexuality.

We're going to consider a few ways to extend these periods. In general most couples spend little time on arousal—ten to fifteen minutes. Then another five to ten minutes in intense sexual activity—the pre-orgasmic stage. A fleeting moment for the orgasm. And the post-orgasmic phase is, essentially, jumping up to bathe or rolling over and going to sleep!

Elsewhere in this book we look at how to extend the arousal phase, something that's especially important for most women's pleasure. But here we want to discuss how to extend the states of extreme arousal. There are several reasons to extend these phases. First, they are extremely pleasurable—so why not get more of that pleasure? Second, the longer you extend this pre-orgasmic stage, the more explosive will be your orgasm. That's wonderful for you, and a great turn-on for your partner to see you there. Some women even play a game in which they extend the man's pre-orgasmic phase as long as possible so they can see just how far or how high his ejaculate can spurt when he finally comes. (The explosiveness of the orgasm after extending pre-orgasm is not purely subjective. In the man's case, at least, you can see clear, objective evidence of heightened orgasmic response.) It's a great turn-on for the man, too, when his partner comes with such force that she's totally out of control. And finally, if you can extend the post-orgasmic phase, you can often bring about more orgasms, and even more pleasure.

So why not spend a sexual session fooling around with your orgasms? Don't simply have intercourse until orgasm, then roll over and go to sleep. Rather, spend some time seeing how long you can each hold out, and how long you can continue the pleasure after the orgasm. Let me explain how.

❧ ❧ Extending a Woman's Pre-Orgasmic (and Orgasmic) Sensation ❧ ❧

With a little communication, you can extend the woman's pre-orgasmic period considerably. In many cases you can also extend the orgasm itself, or quickly bring her to several more orgasms after her first. Spend time kissing and caressing; don't go straight for the genitals, and don't think about intercourse until later! The man should use his hands and mouth to stimulate the woman, starting away from her vagina—her breasts, perhaps, her inner thighs, the buttocks and backs of the legs. Concentrate on her favorite erogenous zones.

When you finally begin stimulating her vaginal lips and clitoris, watch closely for signs that she's nearing orgasm. She should tell you how close she's getting, too. When she's close to having an orgasm, reduce stimulation of the clitoris and let the sensation subside a little, so she doesn't have an orgasm. When it's clear that the moment has passed, resume stimulation. Keep teasing like this, bringing her close and then backing off, as many times as she can stand. When she simply can't stand any more (that will be clear, she'll probably be begging for you to let her come), keep going through the point of pre-orgasm all the way to her orgasm. If you wait too long, she might take things in hand and finish for herself.

After she's had her orgasm—or started her orgasm, that is—you can try to extend the orgasmic pleasure. She may be able to maintain the pleasure of the orgasm for several minutes, or to have several more orgasms. Many women don't want stimulation past the orgasm. In some senses they are like men, who come and then have a "refractory" period during which further stimulation may be uncomfortable. It may take a few minutes for these women to continue with sexual stimulation after an orgasm. Other women, however, want to be stimulated for several minutes straight through the post-orgasmic stage because they can experience a wave of smaller orgasmic after-shocks. A gradually diminishing pressure against a woman's clitoris can slowly bring her to a warm and satisfied state of "completion." Talk about this with your partner, so you both know what she prefers. Of course she can *tell* the man exactly what she wants at the time, too, talking him through the post-orgasmic "procedure" while it is taking place.

When she completes her orgasm the man may try one of these techniques to extend her post-orgasmic pleasure:

- He may provide soft hand pressure (not movement) over the clitoris and insert his finger into her vagina (or insert his penis into her from behind), and stimulate her G spot (we'll talk more about the G spot in Module 28).
- He may maintain a very light manual stroking of her clitoral area, and simultaneously insert his penis into her vagina (again, from the rear, or from the rear side position), to stimulate her outer vaginal opening.
- He may insert his finger into her vagina to stimulate her G spot, while also continuing light stroking of her clitoral area with his tongue and lips.
- He may insert his penis into her vagina, and thrust slowly in a manner that pulls and pushes against the lips of the vagina; he might hold the shaft of the penis so he can control how the head of the penis slips in and out of her between her vaginal lips. Direct clitoral pressure is minimized, but the gentle tugging against the lips and clitoral hood caused by the penis will be pleasurable.
- He may insert his penis into her vagina (from the rear or rear side position) and as he gently caresses her clitoris she may place her fingers parallel and either above or under his fingers to direct his stroking movements.
- He may insert his penis into her vagina (from the rear or rear side position) and with a vibrator on low power he or she gently caresses her clitoris.
- He may insert his penis into her vagina (from the rear or rear side position) and as he gently caresses her clitoris she may place her fingers parallel and either above or under his fingers to direct his stroking movements and to play in the wetness.

One man in our study described how he liked to extend his wife's orgasms. "We have intercourse with her on top until she completes her orgasm. Immediately after, I slide her straight up toward my mouth, insert a finger or two into her vagina and quickly use my tongue in slow, broad circular motions up and down and around her clitoris. I can keep her going for as long as my tongue lasts—it is her favorite because the crawling position allows her to move her hips to meet the pressure of my tongue."

Another man reported a different technique: "I use a vibrator on her clitoris until she orgasms. Immediately after that I mount her 'doggie style' from the rear. At the same time she turns the vibrator onto a low speed and presses it lightly against her outer lips so the sensation will not be too abrasive. The soft vibration follows up to my penis and I come soon after."

✳ ✳ And Now, the Man's Turn . . . ✳ ✳

The principle behind extending the man's pre-orgasmic period is pretty much the same as for the woman; bring him to the brink, then reduce the stimulation. You may be able to play that game without any help—using oral sex, manual stimulation, or intercourse, bring the man to the edge of orgasm, then back off for a few moments and let the feeling subside. When he's no longer close to an orgasm, resume.

For many men, though, this is a hard game to play. They have trouble holding off ejaculation anyway, and they can't last long going to the brink and backing off; they have trouble backing off, and go right on over. If that's a problem for you, see Module 11. In that module we have described a number of techniques that you can use for controlling the man's orgasm, such as *the squeeze, the scrotal tug,* and different positions.

How about extending the orgasm or the post-orgasmic pleasure, though? Immediately following his orgasm a man experiences what's known as the "refractory" period, during which his erection will subside and further stimulation will not immediately cause a new erection—in fact further stimulation may be almost painful, as the head of the penis can become extremely sensitive. (So it's important immediately after orgasm that the woman is careful about the sorts of stimulation she uses—in general, use light strokes.)

Now, this is not true of all men. Some men, particularly younger men, may not even lose their erection after an orgasm, and may be able to continue intercourse almost immediately after orgasm. The sensations will be dulled, and the erection may soften slightly, but these men have little or no refractory period. Most, however, will feel tired after their orgasm, and can easily fall asleep.

What, then, can a woman do to extend her mate's pleasure after orgasm? Here are a few ideas:

- Keep talking to him—don't let him slip into sleep. Encourage him to respond to you, too, or he may simply tune you out!
- After orgasm the penis remains in the vagina—or is placed in the vagina—and the woman contracts her vaginal muscles, squeezing the penis in a slow, sensual rhythm.

- He lies on his back and she mounts him from above, then slowly raises and lowers her hips so that the walls of her vagina completely cover and pull against the head of the penis.
- After an orgasm from oral sex, his penis remains in her mouth, and she very lightly sucks, licks, and runs her tongue around the head of the penis, and along the sides of the shaft.
- She gently sucks the penis while lightly stroking and holding his testicles.
- With her hand she uses her wet fingers to slowly stroke the length of the penis and to make circles around the head of the penis.
- She presses the head of the penis around her vaginal opening and between her moist lips. The movement is slow, gentle, soft, and nonpenetrating.
- She presses his penis against her leg or stomach with her hand, and continues gentle, rhythmic pressing, using the moisture of his ejaculate to rub the penis against her skin.

✣ ✣ Before You Go to Sleep ✣ ✣

When you've finished sexual activity, don't just roll over and go to sleep. This is something that's important for the man to understand, perhaps more than the woman. Women often complain that the man "finishes" and that's it . . . the end of contact. Ninety-eight percent of the women we surveyed greatly enjoy afterplay, and almost all of them stated they did not receive it enough. While men "come down" from their orgasm quite rapidly, women take much longer.

This mismatch of timing leads to problems between many couples. Women often resent the way men finish with them and want to move on . . . to smoke a cigarette, get up and watch TV, go to sleep, or whatever. They end up feeling used, as if the man simply took what he needed and then left them, emotionally and (in some cases) physically.

So, a few words for the man. When you come to the end of your sexual activity, try not to wind down too quickly. If your penis is still inside your partner, leave it there for a little while; there's no rush to pull it out. Continue hugging and kissing affectionately. Talk quietly; tell her you love her, how good the sex was, how much you enjoy making love to her. This afterplay is as much part of extending the good feelings of sex as any of the other techniques we've discussed.

Sexual Position #8

This position provides deep penetration and, because the penis rubs against the front of the vaginal wall, can also stimulate the G spot. Both partners have a degree of control. The man can thrust, and hold the woman's hips to pull her onto his penis. The woman can sway back and forth, and swing her hips from side to side, or even move her buttocks in a rotating motion against the man's groin. The man may also be able to reach her breasts, or at least lean on one hand and squeeze a breast with the other. And he may also be able to reach with one hand under their groins and rub her clitoris and vaginal lips as he thrusts into her.

This position also provides a view that the man will probably find extremely exciting. He may enjoy caressing and squeezing her buttocks and legs while viewing this most sexual of displays.

Module 11

Controlling Orgasm

*P*remature orgasm—every man's nightmare, every man's embarrassment. Virtually every man has at some time come a little sooner than he'd wished or intended. *The Hite Report on Male Sexuality* found that between seventy and eighty percent of men said that at some point in their lives they had lost orgasmic control soon after vaginal penetration. The teenage boy coming as soon as he enters a woman—or even before—is almost a cliché, though it's very common. But it's not just a teenager's problem; for many men it's a continuing problem. They just can't control their orgasms; they seem unable to "keep going" long enough to please their mates. (Actually premature orgasm isn't, in many cases, a "problem." As we'll see in a moment, it's simply an idiosyncrasy that can be handled in a variety of ways.)

But what is premature ejaculation? Just how fast do men come? Here are typical "times to orgasm" from inserting the penis into the vagina until ejaculation:

> One minute or less: 21 percent of men.
> Between one and five minutes: 62 percent of men.
> Five minutes or more: 17 percent of men.

To a great extent, premature ejaculation is a subjective matter. If you think you came too quickly, and if your partner thinks you came too quickly, it might be termed premature ejaculation. So absolute numbers don't mean much. A man who comes very quickly, and has a partner who prefers such brief inter-course, has no problem. A man who holds out much longer—but has a partner who prefers intercourse to last even longer—has more of a problem. Perhaps one man in ten has the condition to such a degree that it causes great frus-tration in his partner, and may threaten his marriage or relationship. But remember that it's not always a simple matter of the man coming too soon. As we've discussed elsewhere in this book, many women are unable to orgasm through intercourse, so however long the man thrusts, she won't reach satis-faction. (If this is your situation, we may be able to help. The position at the end of this module may help.)

Curiously, in our study we found that the wealthier a man is, and the more education he has, the longer he's likely to go before ejaculation. Other researchers support this finding and have suggested that men of limited edu-cation and experience tend to view sex as something for their own pleasure, and may be less concerned with their partner's pleasure.

Now, we've got to admit that we've held something back from you. We told you early in this book that if you eat well, exercise, and avoid drugs, you'll become more interested in sex. And that's quite true. But there's one small problem with this; men who followed our program commented that their penises become much more sensitive to vaginal touch (that's nice!), and by examining their sexual diaries we found that they reduced time to orgasm by 22 percent (maybe not quite so nice). However, forty percent of them were able to achieve a second erection (while before the program they usually had-n't been able to manage this second erection).

✿ ✿ Fun for All ✿ ✿

Now, before you skip this module, thinking "I don't have this problem," or "my man doesn't have premature orgasm," please continue reading. You'll find some techniques that everyone should know, techniques that can be fun whether you "need" them or not. Some of the techniques can be used to extend a man's arousal before orgasm, something that can dramatically increase the power of the orgasm when it finally happens—as we saw in Module 10. So, for all of you— premature ejaculators, partners of premature ejaculators, and all the rest—here are a few techniques you can use.

✿ ✿ Don't Slow Him Down! ✿ ✿

Perhaps the first technique is simply not to worry about it. Let the man come as soon as he wants—or as late as he's able to hold out. His partner can bring him to orgasm with her hand or mouth, or have him come inside her. Then continue with sex. In many cases, particularly if he's a young man, he'll be able to continue immediately or almost immediately; he may not even lose his erection. Other men may take a few minutes to come back, though they can often begin intercourse again before getting a full erection. A partial erection is okay, and it will harden further as he moves.

One man in our study told us: "I usually come within the first fifteen seconds of intercourse, so I simply continue stimulating her clitoris by hand rubbing until my erection returns. Then I'm able to extend thrusting for five to ten minutes before I come the second time." Another said this: "I'm lucky. My wife doesn't orgasm with intercourse, so after I come I simply take care of her any way she wants. That way I can orgasm when I please." These are both great ways to deal with this "problem"—by not regarding it as a problem!

The Hite Report on Male Sexuality found that forty percent of men who tried to have a second orgasm were successful, and that the second orgasm was significantly weaker. However, we found in our studies that most of the men who had more than one orgasm during a single sexual encounter tended to be aerobic exercisers under the age of thirty-five; only about five percent of men over fifty claimed to have two, sometimes three, orgasms. That doesn't mean more men couldn't though. Undoubtedly many men don't because they've fallen into the "one orgasm then off to sleep" syndrome. In any case, if you are concerned about bringing pleasure to your partner, you may get satisfaction from simply being able to continue intercourse after your first orgasm, whether or not you have a second. And if you can't retain an erection, you can still bring pleasure to your partner with your mouth and hands, any number of ways.

The second orgasm will take longer, perhaps much longer. While he may be a first-orgasm premature ejaculator, the second (and subsequent) orgasms will be much delayed. However, there's a problem with this method for many men. Once the orgasm is over, your brain is flooded with chemicals that say, in effect, "Go to sleep!" We've all experienced the sudden feeling of well being and exhaustion immediately after an orgasm. What can you do? You can simply train yourself to get through it. Force yourself awake, start moving inside the vagina again, and within a few minutes you'll be fully alert. This is something you can learn to do, and the more you do it the easier it will become.

✶ ✶ Pre-Sex Masturbation ✶ ✶

Some men masturbate half an hour or an hour before they have sex. This is the same as the method we just described, of course—the second orgasm will be less intense and will be delayed. Why bother masturbating, though, when you could come during sex and then come again? Some men may want to masturbate if they feel embarrassed by their early ejaculation—though perhaps they should talk with their partners about it—or with a new partner.

Controlling Orgasm

(With a new partner you may be able to take a quick trip to the bathroom and masturbate a few minutes before sex! On the other hand, you might find that discussing the situation with her may be a better, more honest thing to do.)

✳ ✳ Stop Thrusting ✳ ✳

As you've learned elsewhere in this book, a woman doesn't require constant thrusting to find pleasure in intercourse. If you are about to come, stop thrusting for a few moments. Change the pace; kiss her deeply, lie together and caress her buttocks and back, press your groin into hers in a churning motion. Ask your partner to relax her vaginal muscles, and to stop moving on your penis. You can even completely withdraw, if you wish. Then, when the feeling of impending orgasm has subsided, continue. You can stop and start several times; you'll eventually learn to control orgasm and hold off for extended periods.

✳ ✳ Change Positions ✳ ✳

A simple method for extending orgasm that works for some couples is to change positions. Let the woman get on top. The missionary position is one of the worst positions you can use if the man has trouble controlling orgasm. When the woman is in the position shown at the end of Module 9—the *oceanic* position—the tension in the man's pubococcygeus and thrusting muscles is greatly reduced, in turn reducing the ejaculatory urge. She may get more stimulation out of the position, too, as she can position her clitoris against his pubic bone while she moves her hips, and he can use his hands to caress the pubic mound and clitoris.

✳ ✳ Try It From Behind ✳ ✳

Another change in position might prove helpful. Try a few rear positions—the "doggie" position, with the woman on her hands and knees, or the "spoon," with both partners lying on their sides. Slow thrusts can be made against sensual counterthrusts by the woman, and the hands are left free for caresses, especially clitoral stimulation.

✳ ✳ The Scrotal Tug ✳ ✳

Now we get to the real fun. In this method, as the male is about to come, one of you grasps around the top of the testicles and tugs down on them. This is a powerful way to stop orgasm—if you've never tried it you might be surprised at the effect.

Try this little experiment. The man lies on his back while his partner kneels or lies in front of him or beside him. She then uses the thumb and forefinger of one hand to grasp the skin of the scrotum—the "ball sack"—immediately above the testicles themselves. That is, the fingers create a ring squeezing the skin of the scrotum together, between the underside of the penis and the testicles themselves, as shown in the following illustration.

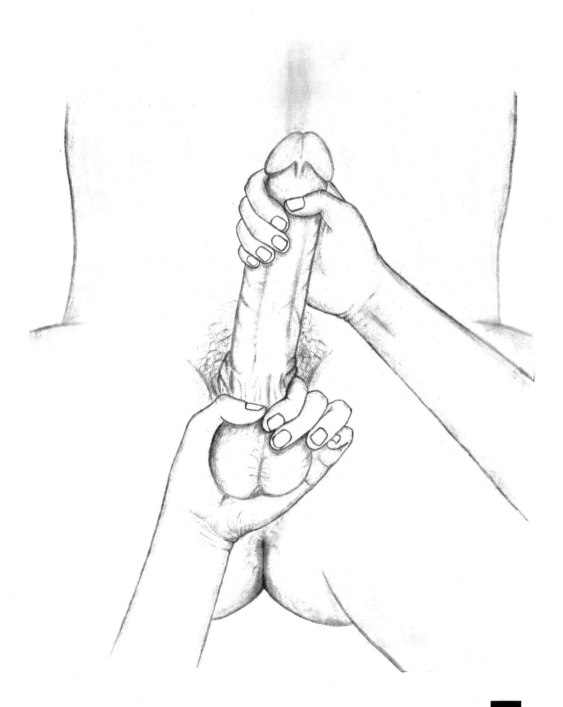

Controlling Orgasm

Now, this is sometimes difficult to do if he already has an erection; it's easier if he hasn't yet hardened, because there's more "sag" to grasp. If he's already erect, though, she can pull slowly, tugging a little, and gradually work her fingers between the testicles and his body, until she can get her fingers all the way around.

Now that she has him, what to do with him? Well, she tugs down slowly. The tug inhibits orgasm if applied before the orgasm begins. (If the orgasm is in progress there's no stopping it even if she swings on his testicles like Tarzan.) The woman may try to masturbate him with one hand, give his penis an oil massage, or suck him. And every time he's about to reach an orgasm, tug down on his testicles to stop the orgasm. When the sensation subsides, resume stimulation.

This is a great game for *any* couple, not simply for couples who think they're premature ejaculators. You can continue this way for hours—as long as the woman can last, anyway. When you finally allow him to come, his orgasm will be extraordinarily powerful.

To use this technique to prolong intercourse, you may have to experiment to find a position in which you can use the tug. He may be able to tug on his testicles himself in some positions, but in general the woman can gently tug more easily. The position we looked at in Module 6 (the *scissors*) allows the woman to reach between his legs and grasp him, for instance. But there's another method of applying the tug. You can get a strap that's designed for this very purpose (see Module 17 for a list of places where you can buy one). You put the strap on before your erection, and leave it there until you are ready to come—the strap, in effect, applies a permanent tug. Then quickly remove it when you are ready to come (it's probably fastened with Velcro!) and away you go.

The Squeeze

Another manual technique for slowing ejaculation is known as the squeeze. The woman should place her thumb on the frenulum of the penis (that is, the small area of skin on the underside of the penis, where the head of the penis—the glans—joins the shaft of the penis), her index finger above and the middle finger below the coronal ridge of the head of the penis. She can use one or both hands.

When you tell her to squeeze, she applies a firm grasping pressure for five seconds, and then releases. Try the squeeze with the woman masturbating the penis to a point of near ejaculation—then squeeze to stop the ejaculation. Practice the squeeze a few times, until you both feel confident with it. Then try it during intercourse, like this:

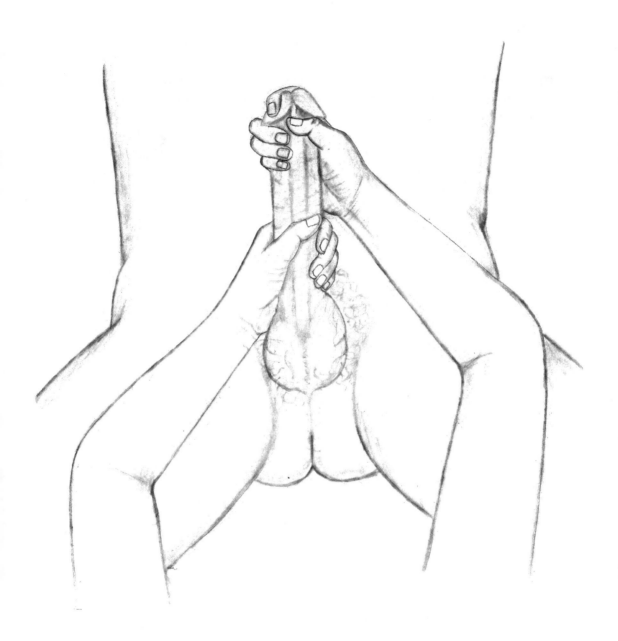

When the man feels that he's about to come, he withdraws his penis, she grasps the penis and, at his command "squeeze," applies the appropriate pressure for five seconds and then releases. Some couples use several of these squeezes in quick succession to drive away strong orgasmic sensation. Then reinsert the penis and continue thrusting.

This technique may take some practice, and will quite likely fail the first few times you try it; the pressure may be too light, painfully strong (though that's more likely to stop the erection than to induce orgasm), or because the timing was wrong. Continue trying to perfect the technique, though, and gradually the number of times the man has to remove his penis to get a squeeze will be reduced. In *Human Sexual Inadequacy*, Masters and Johnson claim that ninety-seven percent of all men trying this method can recondition their orgasmic response.

There's a similar technique you can try—the *basilar squeeze*. The woman uses her thumb and first two fingers to grasp the penis where it attaches to the body. She holds the squeeze for five seconds and then releases. The success rate is similar to the squeeze technique described above.

✳ ✳ Forget the Penis ✳ ✳

Another way to handle premature ejaculation is to make sex less "penis-centric." Throughout this book we've told you about other ways to please a woman—massage, oral sex, manual stimulation, long and sensual arousal. You don't *need* a penis to bring pleasure to a woman. Spend more time on other sexual activities, and she'll still be happy, even if you come quickly when you finally do get to intercourse.

✳ ✳ Try an Analgesic Cream . . . or a Condom ✳ ✳

Many sex catalogs and shops sell special creams designed to slow the man down. They contain analgesics that deaden the sensation on the penis for twenty or thirty minutes, and they really can work. However, they can deaden the vagina and clitoris, too! So if you want to try one of these creams, apply the cream and then slip on a condom. In fact, you might try the condom without the analgesic cream. Some men find that a thick condom is all it takes to slow them down.

✳ ✳ Deep Breathing ✳ ✳

Some therapists believe that deep breathing may help to relax you and reduce involuntary ejaculatory response. Taking a few deep breaths decreases carbon dioxide in the blood and reduces tension. So slow your thrusting now and again and take a few deep breaths. (But warn your partner first, or she may think you are having a seizure . . . or the Mother of all Orgasms!)

✳ ✳ Cross-Sensory Masking ✳ ✳

Cross-Sensory Masking is a fancy name for thinking about something else while you are performing a task. Many men try this little trick—it's a common joke among men, in fact. ("If I'm about to come, I think about baseball!") Just about anything will do. Think about work, about household chores, about a trip you are planning. Try to take your mind away from the sex, and let your body carry on with the work! Some men try to think about things that are particularly unpleasant—pain, accidents, and so on. This can work well, though it's a shame to have to introduce such unpleasantness into something that should be so good.

Some men apply some kind of physical pain to really get their mind off the orgasm! "I place both hands under the pillow above her head and quietly dig the fingernail of one thumb into the fingers of the opposite hand," one man in our study told us. "The closer to coming, the more pressure and pain I exert. Then if I come close to losing my erection less pressure and pain are exerted." Other men focus concentration on a different body part, so they notice the sensation in their penis less.

✵ ✵ PC-Muscle Control ✵ ✵

In Module 1 we looked at Kegel exercises, a technique for working the PC (pubococcygeus) muscles. We have no definitive proof, but we believe that strengthening the PC muscles may improve orgasmic control. Some men report that contracting the PC muscles ten times, three times each day, and five days of the week, helps them control ejaculation—as well as providing more intense orgasms.

✵ ✵ Practice When You Are On Your Own! ✵ ✵

In the movie *Love and Death,* a beautiful woman tells Woody Allen that he's a wonderful lover. "Oh, I practice a lot when I'm on my own," he responds. Well, you may find that practicing on your own—masturbating, that is—can help you control your ejaculations. Most sex therapists believe that ejaculatory control can be learned through masturbation.

Here's your task: Masturbate four to seven times a week, and keep a stop watch next to you! The first week you must masturbate exactly five minutes before ejaculating. The second week, go to six minutes, and so on. Keep "training" like this until you can reach twenty to thirty minutes before your orgasm.

Focus your attention on the feeling in your penis. Certain areas feel more sensitive. Pay attention to the especially good feelings that lead up to orgasm, and as the sensation peaks, slow your stroking, reduce the pressure, and move your hand away from the sensitive head of the penis toward the less sensitive base. When the feeling of impending orgasm subsides, return to full pressure, and to the head of the penis.

Don't worry if you misjudge things and come too soon. That's okay, just try again the next day. Incidentally, learning to delay orgasm in this way has a great little side effect. You'll find that your orgasms are much more intense and pleasurable.

✻ ✻ Create an Incentive Plan ✻ ✻

Here's a nice idea—the woman should give the man an incentive for lasting longer! Incentives have been proven to help change habits in many areas of life, and sex is no different. Here's a plan you can use. The man has to play a little ejaculation-control game, and if he wins, he gets a prize. If he loses, his partner gets a prize. We'll look at the game, and then at the prizes you can win. So *Contestant number one, come on down!*

Start with the woman using her hand to stimulate the penis. She strokes the penis, trying to bring her partner to orgasm. When the orgasm is imminent, he asks her to stop. She looks at the clock or a stop watch, and observes how long she stroked his penis before he asked her to stop. Once the pre-orgasm sensation has subsided, she continues. The man tries to extend the time before he has to ask her to stop—he might try focusing on another part of his body or thinking about football scores, whatever it takes to increase that time. Do ten "rounds" and then continue with any sexual activity you want.

The next phase of the game, once you've played the hand game for a couple of weeks, is to use intercourse. With the man on his back, the woman straddles him and inserts his penis into her vagina. When he says he's ready, she makes deep, slow vertical thrusts along the full length of his penis. When the man feels that he is about to come, he tells her to stop. Again, she checks the time, and try to increase the time before telling her to stop. Play ten rounds, then continue with any sexual activity you choose.

Later, when the man has improved ejaculatory control using the woman-on-top position, try the same game with the missionary position. This time, of course, it's up to the man to stop when he feels the need. Now, how do you win? The first time you play, there's no prize. The next time you play (play one to three times a week), if the man doubles his average times from the previous week, he wins the game. If he doesn't, the woman wins. And what might be awarded as prizes? Well, use your imagination. Anything, sexual or nonsexual. If you are the winner, you might get:

- Oral sex.
- A complete body massage.
- A favorite sexual act that you rarely indulge in.
- Your partner to do a household chore that you normally do.
- A piece of clothing, a book, or another prize of your choice.

Okay, it's just a game. But it's a way to introduce a little fun into an exercise that teaches ejaculation control.

❧ ❧ Find a Sex Therapist ❧ ❧

Many men can learn to slow down a little, if they just try. But if you have a particularly intractable problem, you may want to see a sex therapist and get professional help. You can ask your doctor for a referral, or find a therapist in the yellow pages.

Sexual Position #9

Here's a position that is rarely described in the sex literature, yet can be very effective for helping the man reach ejaculatory control *and* satisfy his partner. We've called it the "ultimate" position. It seems to be new to the United States. It was first illustrated by a Japanese painter named Eisen [1790–1848]. We believe that this is one of the best ways to assure female orgasm during intercourse, while allowing almost complete ejaculatory control by the man. And although virtually every movement in this position is dominated and controlled by the man, don't be surprised if this position becomes everyone's favorite!

The man lies by his partner's right side (if he is right-handed) and arouses her clitoris to near orgasm with his fingers, as you can see in the following illustration. For extended "finger play" he can lie a little higher and more on his back—he may get too tired in the position shown otherwise.

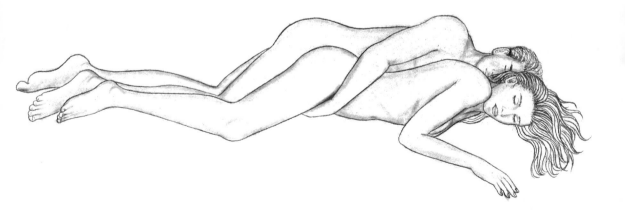

When she approaches orgasm, she rolls to her left (face down and nearly flat) and keeps her right hip and pubic area raised just enough to allow her partner to freely maintain clitoral stroking with his right hand as he rolls on top of her. She needs to raise her pubic area up so as to lessen the weight on her lover's arm and hand. He's not going to be much use if the blood to his arm is cut off!

Without interrupting the clitoral caresses he can insert his penis when he is ready. Also, she can reach under and back between her legs to touch his testicles, and to insert him if she wants to do so. He continues hand stroking until she indicates that her orgasm is complete. He can come anytime he wishes. During thrusting he can regulate his orgasm to coincide with hers or he can withdraw to avoid early ejaculation. If he comes before she has finished he can continue clitoral stimulation—he can withdraw his penis and replace it with a finger or, better yet, his thumb, which is in perfect position to stimulate her G spot (see Module 28). If you have a vibrator, you could use that instead.

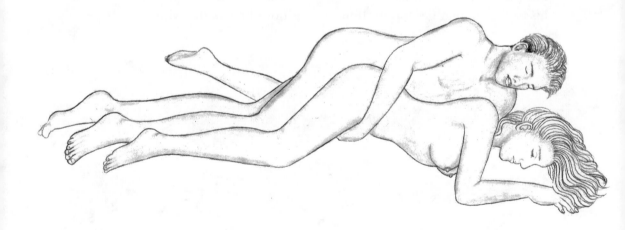

Module 12

Massage, The Woman's Turn

assage. It's relaxing, it feels good, and it's very sexy. Massage can be extremely erotic. It doesn't need to start out that way, but the feeling of your partner's hands as they rub your body and squeeze your muscles can be very pleasing and very sensual. A massage can begin by being a truly innocent body rub intended to relax you, and gradually turn into something much more exciting.

Why not take turns with massage? Do one of you tonight and the other tomorrow, or even both on the same night if you have the stamina. You may find, though, that done right the massage will take a while and lead directly into sex, so you may not want to start over again. It's perhaps better to do one massage per night. Let's start tonight with her, and the man can have his turn tomorrow (see the following module).

Massage has a couple of distinct advantages. First, it tends to focus your attention on your body. Rather than rushing straight to intercourse, concentrating on the sexual feeling based in the genitalia, massage reminds you that there's more to your bodies than what's between your legs, and teaches you that sensual pleasure can be derived from just about any body part that is touched. Also, it's the perfect arousal technique for a woman. Women typically complain that their partners ignore or limit arousal, and are too interested in getting to intercourse. Massage can provide the intimacy and closeness that women enjoy and so often don't get.

You may want to start by placing several large towels or a large soft blanket over the bed; you're going to be using oil or lotion, which will feel great during massage and sex, but a little slimy when sleeping! You may also want another large towel available for wiping your hands. You can buy massage oils from many places; from health-food stores, some drug stores, the catalogs mentioned in Module 17, local sex-toy stores, on the Internet, from The Body Shop, and so on. If you don't have any massage oil available, you could make do with some kind of body lotion or moisturizer, or a vegetable oil such as coconut oil. Try a real massage oil sometime, though; they are often scented, and the fragrance adds to the sensual atmosphere. Some partners enjoy using various materials to rub over the skin, too, such as silk and large feathers. You might want to burn a little incense, to add to the atmosphere.

By the way, while most massage oils probably won't taste too good, it's possible to find flavored oils (try the sex catalogs and sex shops). If you think you'll be using your mouth as a massage tool, you might want to try flavored oils.

Find some suitable way to apply the oil; you might use it straight from the bottle, or perhaps from a bowl (make sure you don't spill it). You'll probably want to warm the oil before you start.

Begin with the woman face down on the bed. Then try the following procedure, which describes a massage developing into an *erotic* massage. Take your time on the massage basics—there's no rush to get to the genitals, so make sure you spend enough time working on the rest of your partner's body:

1. Start by massaging her shoulders, the base of the neck, the sides of the neck, and up into the hairline at the back of the head. Begin lightly rubbing oil into the skin, then gradually intensify the pressure by working your fingers firmly and deeply into the muscles. Ask her what feels good. Some people enjoy a really deep, almost painful massage . . . it's a great way to release tension in the muscles. Others prefer a lighter touch, what massage therapists who do very deep work sometimes call a "fluffing" massage; it won't do much to release deep tensions, but can feel good at the surface level.

2. Use gentle kneading motions with your hands, alternating with circular motions, on the neck, shoulders, back, and arms.

3. Place the hands on her back, with thumbs together, hands pointing up toward her head. Then move the hands in opposite directions, one rubbing up toward her head, the other down to the base of her spine. Then reverse directions.

4. Rub down to the lower back and out to the waist. Use gentle pressure with your fingers on the abdominal area and the sides of her hips.

5. Place a drop of oil on each buttock, and use a circular motion to rub the oil into the skin. Rub around onto the sides of the buttocks, then down

over the buttocks to the tops of the legs. As you slide your hands down the backs of her legs you might slip your thumbs between her legs, and gently touch where the crease of the buttocks and the lips of the vagina meet. (Don't spend too much time doing this, though. You should be merely teasing her, not forgetting about the massage!)

6. Now move down the backs of her legs, pausing momentarily on the backs of the knees. Rub and squeeze the calves, ankles, and the bottom of the feet—use a firm motion on the feet, because you don't want to tickle. That might cause her to lose the sensual mood.

7. Turn her onto her back.

8. Straddle her hips, facing toward her head. Or try kneeling between her open legs. You might also try kneeling at her head, with her head between your legs. Try a few positions, and see which is the most comfortable or appropriate for a particular stroke you want to use.

9. Rub oil slowly between her breasts and along the sides of her ribs with soft strokes. Then rub the oil into each breast in turn, lingering if her response indicates that she likes it.

10. Lightly caress her stomach, along the fronts of her thighs, and gently tease the vaginal area.

11. Massage down the fronts of her thighs and the sides of her hips, go to the knees, then drop down to the front of the lower leg, the ankles, the feet, and finally the toes.

12. Spend some time massaging the inner thighs and behind the knees, very sensitive areas for a woman.

13. Move slowly up toward the vaginal area, rubbing warm oil onto the insides of her calves, knees, and inner thighs. Try gentle nibbles on her legs one or two inches above the kneecaps and on the inner thigh—this stimulates a sexual reflex.

14. Move up along the inner thighs and then circle slowly around the pubic hair and the outside of the vaginal lips.

15. Ask your partner to open her legs a little. Pour a little oil on your fingers and rub vertically along her vaginal lips. Gently part the lips with your fingers, and run your fingers along the inner lips up to and over the top of her clitoris. Avoid the clitoris for a few moments, as you rub back down again, then move back up and touch the clitoris fleetingly.

16. After a few moments begin very lightly caressing the clitoris; add a drop more oil if necessary. You might use your other hand to continue massaging the vaginal lips, or even insert a finger or two. Ask her, "How does that feel?" and respond accordingly. She may want you to back off a little, and continue massaging her body. Or she may be quite ready for what you have started.

17. As you continue massaging her clitoris and vaginal lips, you could try to massage the G spot (we'll discuss this in more detail in Module 28). It's on the front wall of the vagina, about two inches or so inside. Try rubbing with the flats of the fingers that you have inside her against the wall of the vagina, and ask her to direct you to the position. As the G spot is stimulated, it should grow harder and larger. (You'll need relatively firm strokes on the G spot, not the light strokes that you would use on her clitoris.)

18. With your fingers inside her, rubbing the G spot, place the other hand on her abdomen with the fingers down on the clitoris. Try a rocking motion, as your oiled hand rocks forward, pushing down on the abdomen slightly and rubbing the clitoris with your fingers, and then back.

19. Be aware of your partner's reactions and respond accordingly. She may want you to bring her to orgasm in this manner, rubbing her clitoris with one hand and her G spot with the other. This is likely to produce a very intense orgasm. Or perhaps she'd prefer that you use your mouth at this point (though, depending on the type and amount of oil you've been using, that may not be pleasant for you). You might try using a vibrator inside her, while you continue using a hand to rub oil onto her clitoris and vaginal lips. Or maybe she'd prefer that you enter her . . . try angling your pelvis so that your pubic bone presses against her clitoral area.

When you've finished the massage, feel free to indulge in intercourse. Ah, but you don't need to be told that. If you've gone all the way through this body massage, you'll have trouble *avoiding* intercourse. Enjoy the feeling of your bodies slipping over each other, providing a new and exciting sensation. It's not only fun, but a great way to moisturize dry skin!

There are many ways to massage your partner. Why not try the following module, and give the man a turn? We'll discuss some other techniques that can be used on either partner in that module.

Sexual Position #10

This is a nice position in which you can continue the massage. The man is able to continue rubbing the oil into her skin on her legs, buttocks, and breasts. He may even be able to continue rubbing her clitoris and vaginal lips. Try different positions for the woman's legs; if her thighs remained pressed together, it will produce a nice tight fit for his penis. Put one leg on each shoulder for a different sensation and view.

Module 13

Massage— The Man's Turn

If you enjoyed Module 12, why not continue with massage and try another little session . . . this time it's the man's turn to lie down and relax. One nice thing about massaging each other is that each of you can learn what the other likes. If your partner tries something on you, there's a good chance that it's something he or she would like you to try, too. So when you massage each other, pay attention, notice what your partner is doing, and don't be afraid to suggest something that might feel nice; "massage my thighs," "squeeze tighter," or "use your knuckles on my back," for instance. Remember that it's very difficult for the person who is massaging to know exactly the pressure and type of stroke that feels good. What's a good firm stroke for one person, is too light to bother with for another. So let your partner know what you like.

Massaging a man is really similar to massaging a woman . . . with important differences, of course. Begin with some of the preliminaries suggested in Module 12. Then there are a few little specialties that a woman can use on her man. He'll probably enjoy having his body stroked with your hair; he'll almost certainly enjoy having it stroked by your breasts. Try positioning yourself on your hands and knees over your partner, so that you can rub your nipples lightly along his back and buttocks, or over his chest. You might move all the way up his body, rubbing his penis, belly, and chest, and allowing a nipple to gently drop into his mouth at the end of the run (you'll probably find that it's open and quite eager to be filled!). Why not try placing a drop or two of oil on your partner, and then use your breasts to rub the oil in? Or use your breasts to brush against his nipples.

When you've spent some time working on his body, and you get to the point when you want to massage his penis, you could use a variety of techniques:

- Kneel beside him, facing his feet, and rub oil over his testicles and penis. Place your hand over his testicles, with the fingers below them on the perineum (the spot between the testicles and the anus), and rub the oil upward, over his testicles and penis. Use one hand after another, getting a constant motion going. As you pass your hand over his penis, grasp it gently and pull up the shaft.
- "Bathe" the testicles in oil in the palm of your hand, then pull gently on the testicles and let them slip out of your hand.
- Use one hand to pull the skin and foreskin down the shaft of the penis; use the other hand to rub oil onto the head of the penis, moving the tips of your fingers up and down over the head.
- With the head of the penis well oiled, pull down on the shaft of the penis with one hand, while you twist around the head of the penis with your other hand. (Don't expect him to take much of this!)
- Put a few large drops of oil into the palm of your hand, then rub up and down the shaft of the penis while you pull down on the shaft with your other hand.
- Kneel next to him, facing his feet, and oil his inner thighs. Place your hands well down between his thighs, then pull them up, squeezing his thighs as you go, and rubbing his testicles and penis with your thumbs as your hands come out.

❊ ❊ More Techniques You Can Both Use ❊ ❊

Remember there's no reason to limit yourself to one or two techniques. The idea is to stimulate your partner's body through touch. That touch may come from hands gently rubbing, or from a mouth kissing, a tongue licking, teeth gently nibbling. Here are a few more ways to stimulate your partner:

- Use light, broad gliding motions with your hands over your partner's body. A good way to start a massage, and often used by massage therapists to finish a massage, too. (Though you'll likely be skipping that step!)
- Gentle kneading. Carefully squeeze a handful of flesh as if you were kneading dough.

- Rubbing with the knuckles. Use the knuckles to gently rub in circles.
- Lightly pinch small areas of skin.
- Cup your hands and gently slap your partner's skin, making a light popping sound.
- "Wring" your partner's skin. For instance, use the flat of your hands on your partner's back. Move one hand one direction, the other in the other direction, so the skin is twisted between the two directions.
- Turn your hands over and gently "pummel" a fleshy area of your partner's body.
- Nibble an area; you might choose to nibble your partner's belly, or the backs of the legs, for instance. (Hint: Nibble *before* applying the massage oil, unless you are using the flavored stuff!)
- Don't forget your tongue; try firm swipes with the broad surface of the tongue over the nipples, for example.
- Blow lightly over a sensitive area—such as the backs of the thighs and knees, or the nipples.
- Try breathing warm air over sensitive areas.
- Suck areas of skin into your mouth and then release them. Or suck some flesh into your mouth and hold it there while you rub your tongue over it.
- Use your elbow to knead such an area as the buttocks. Massage therapists often run the elbow down each side of the spine, though you should be very careful not to press too hard if you try this.
- The man could use his penis and testicles to rub various areas, in the way that a woman uses her breasts.
- Use your entire body as an instrument, rubbing yourself over your partner's body. Enjoy the slippery feeling as your bodies slide together.
- Tug gently on your partner's pubic hair.

As you try each technique, you'll learn what your partner enjoys. Begin using each technique quite gently . . . a sudden intense pinch, for instance, is likely to shock your partner. If a technique you've tried produces pleasure, then you can gradually try a firmer or deeper motion. Don't be afraid to ask if your partner wants more pressure. If you think something might feel good, try it. You never know, you might find something that will drive your partner wild.

Sexual Position #11

An interesting position, shown on the following page, but will you manage it? Maybe, with time and practice. If you *can* manage it, then the woman has an rather unusual view of her partner, and can continue massaging oil into his buttocks and the backs of his legs, and even his testicles and anus.

Here's how to get into this position. Start in the normal "missionary" position, with the woman on her back and the man on top. The woman puts her legs down flat on the bed, while the man moves his torso to one side of her, and puts his legs to the other side of her. Take care to keep the penis inside. The man can quickly move around until the two bodies make a cross; the man is lying directly across the woman, at a right angle to her body. If you've never tried this position, you may be surprised at how easy it is to achieve. Yes, the penis really can work sideways! If this is as far as you get, it can still be quite pleasant; the woman can massage oil into his buttocks, and legs, and back.

With practice the man *may* be able to continue spinning around slowly, until his head is between her legs, and her head between his. You are not going to do any vigorous thrusting in this position. This is the sort of position that might be best described with the phrase, "traveling is more important than arriving." It's simply a fun thing to try (sex, remember, is supposed to be about fun).

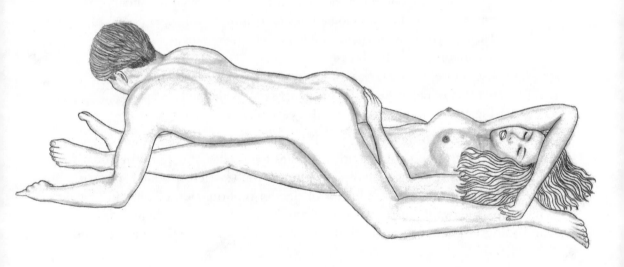

Let's Watch

It's often difficult for men and women to know what their partners really enjoy sexually. In many cases they use what has worked in the past, and their partners, because they find talking about sex difficult and don't want to upset their mate, never really explain what they enjoy, and why what their mate is doing isn't working so well.

If it's difficult for you to know exactly how your partner enjoys being stimulated, remember that there's someone who can *show you* precisely what your partner likes. Who? Your partner, of course. It's almost certain that your partner has masturbated in the past, and in spite of the fact that your partner is now in a relationship with you, he or she almost certainly continues to masturbate when alone, whether you know it or not.

✻ ✻ Masturbation— Don't Believe the Lies ✻ ✻

First, let's get a few things straight about masturbation. It's perfectly natural. In fact, it's hard to understand how anyone can call something that is so widely practiced "unnatural." Children do it, adults do it, even animals do it. American psychiatrist Thomas Szasz has called it the "primary sexual activity of mankind." He observed, "In the nineteenth century it was a disease; in the twentieth, it's a cure." It may have been *considered* a disease, but the truth is that it can't do any harm. Masturbating can't cause physical or emotional problems (obsessive masturbation may in rare cases be related to emotional problems—but it's a symptom of those problems, not a cause). You won't go blind, mad, or grow hair on the palms of your hands.

Still, for most of us it's an embarrassing subject. We don't want to admit that we do it, let alone do it in front of someone else. But let's face it, the chances are you are already doing things in bed that are highly intimate—it's hard to imagine anything more private than oral sex, for instance.

Talk to your partner about this, and you may find that he or she is turned on by the idea of mutual masturbation, or at least willing to try. Explain that it's a way to learn more about each other, about what feels good sexually. And you can find ways to integrate it into your sex life. For instance, the woman might do a striptease, something many women do; the man can lie on the bed and masturbate while watching. Or you can begin with oral sex, and punctuate it with short periods of masturbation. The man might begin performing cunnilingus, for example, and when he gets tired kneel back and watch his partner masturbate for a minute or two. Same for the woman; she can perform fellatio, then rest while he masturbates. You may also find it easier to masturbate in front of each other when already highly aroused, after you've been playing for a while. And while it's nice to simply sit back and watch your partner masturbate, so you can pay complete attention, it might be easier if you both masturbate at the same time, in positions where you can view each other. In positions in which you can touch each other, too; there's no reason why your hand can't slip from your genitals (or other erogenous zones) across to your lover's body now and again.

Masturbating like this is *not* a one-person sex act. While you masturbate you are also, in effect, performing a sexual act on your partner. Your partner will almost certainly get very turned on by watching you, so it's not a matter of you bringing pleasure to yourself while your partner waits and impassively watches. It's all part of sexually arousing your lover. And the benefits you will accrue, as your partner watches and learns, will greatly outweigh any initial trepidation you may experience.

Sexual Position #12

Don't forget to use props in your sex play; nobody said that bed was the only place you can have sex. (Okay, that's not quite true; in fact in some parts of the United States there are *laws* saying that the bed is the only place you can have sex. Still, they are hard to enforce, so you can probably ignore them.)

Use furniture to lean on, to lift legs over, to hold onto, and so on. In this position the woman can both lean on a chair and rest her leg on the chair, opening herself widely to her lover.

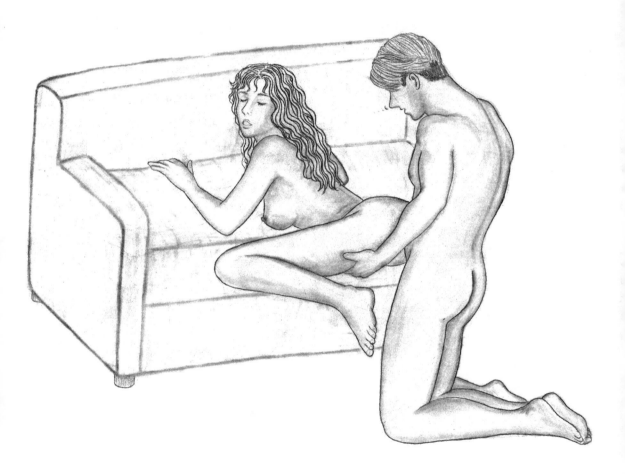

Module 15

Orgasm During Intercourse

In this module we're going to look at a technique that can be used to bring a woman to orgasm during intercourse. It's very common for women to state that although they enjoy intercourse intensely, they can't have an orgasm that way; they require manual stimulation or oral sex for an orgasm. The pleasure a woman feels when she has her clitoris stimulated is similar to what a man enjoys when his penis is stimulated. Vaginal stimulation alone, for most women, is similar to the pleasure a man experiences when he has his testicles caressed. Nice, but not quite nice enough.

That's not a problem, that's just the way it is. We have so many preconceptions about what sex is and should be, but there are no rules. The fact is, most women cannot orgasm through intercourse, or have great difficulty doing so—some studies suggest that only about thirty percent of women can have an orgasm through intercourse alone. However, because many people feel that a woman *should* have an orgasm through intercourse (intercourse is "real" sex, after all, while the rest is just play), the result is that many women feel cheated, and many men feel inadequate. Bad feelings are compounded by the idea that the very best form of orgasm is mutual orgasm—both partners experiencing the orgasm at the same time. While that can be very pleasurable, it can also be difficult for many couples to attain, physically impossible in some cases.

There's no reason to feel cheated or inadequate about biology! Masters and Johnson found that the most intense orgasms, for both women *and* men, are achieved through oral and manual stimulation. That's the way we are built, and it makes no sense to wish that it were otherwise. Still, if you'd like to try an exercise that may lead to an orgasm through intercourse, read on. (And if you can already orgasm through intercourse, read on too—you'll find it's fun.)

It's ironic that in many couples the man spends a few minutes in "foreplay" stimulating the clitoris . . . so that there's enough vaginal lubrication for him to enter her, usually in a position that doesn't stimulate the clitoris! Many sexual positions do not place the pressure on the clitoris that is required to bring the woman to orgasm. One possibility is to bring the woman as close to orgasm as possible using oral and manual techniques, and then begin intercourse using a position that, hopefully, places pressure on the clitoral area. Some couples can pull it off, others cannot.

The Triple Thrusting Theory

There are basically three methods of penile thrusting during intercourse:

- Full thrusting: Long, deep, full-length penile thrusts that stimulate the vaginal opening and sides of the vagina. This method feels great to the penis, and generally produces a firm erection and an orgasm for the male. However, it probably *won't* provide enough clitoral pressure to bring about female orgasm.
- Pressure thrusting: Short-length thrusting with near-constant pubic pressure against the clitoris. This is designed to stimulate the clitoris and, to a lesser degree, the vaginal opening and walls. This can be quite stimulating for the woman, and is relatively effective in producing an orgasm for her. It also may reduce penile sensation, which can be an added benefit, as it will allow better control of the man's orgasm, particularly useful for a man who tends to come very quickly.
- Fixed thrusting: With the man on top, the penis is inserted into the vagina and constant pressure is applied against the clitoris with the man's pubic bone. She can direct the man's body position and pubic pressure to produce the most pleasant sensations. He can use his abdominal muscles to flex his torso such that his pubic bone "plows" a pressure furrow against the vaginal opening and upon the woman's clitoris. That is, he is using his pubic bone to rub against her clitoris while he, in effect, "churns" his penis inside her.

The last position is the one that is most likely to lead to the woman's orgasm. It might be tried with the woman on top, too. The woman can move herself into the best position, the one in which her clitoris is up against the man's pubic bone.

Another method that might be used is for the man to enter the woman from behind; while she lies on a pillow with a vibrator pressed against her clitoris. This position is often very pleasurable for a woman, because the penis rubs against the G spot. Combined with a vibrator it can be quite intense.

Can We Do It Together?— Simultaneous Orgasm

Simultaneous orgasm is like peace on earth; a great idea, but not easy to attain. If you can manage it, it's very pleasurable. But don't feel that you *have* to both orgasm at the same time. In fact even couples that are able to time their sexual responses perfectly and have a simultaneous orgasm every time, don't. Sometimes it's better to just focus on your own orgasm for that moment.

The nonthrusting orgasm we discussed can be used in an attempt to reach simultaneous orgasm. Its great advantage is that it reduces the stimulation on the penis. While the man can rub the pubic bone against the clitoral area, he's not getting the sort of stimulation provided by more active thrusting motions. So it may be possible for a couple to bring the woman to her orgasm with this position and then, as the woman reaches her orgasm, for the man to change to a deeper thrusting motion that brings him to his orgasm. And, with luck, he'll get to his before she finishes hers! (But sometimes he won't; so try, try, and try again.)

Or don't try to match the orgasms the first time. Why not bring the woman to an orgasm alone the first time? Then let the man use one of the deeper thrusting motions that feel so good to him. Many women enjoy the vaginal stimulation of deep intercourse after their orgasm. And in some cases she may sneak a second little orgasm in, too, perhaps at the point of the man's climax.

She Always Comes . . .

Some women come through intercourse virtually all the time. Couples in this happy situation have a different problem, though. They may get complacent, relying on intercourse alone to give the woman pleasure. Why not try a little variety? Allow her to experience orgasm achieved through oral or manual stimulation, or with a vibrator. Variety, remember, keeps sex exciting.

Sexual Position #13

Here's the position we talked of earlier in this module, in which the couple's pubic bone and clitoral area are in contact, providing both vaginal and clitoral stimulation. This is essentially the missionary position, but with the woman's hips on a pillow or two, raising her pubic area up to meet the man's. The woman can move her body to make the best contact against her clitoris, while the man can make sure he moves so that he not only thrusts his penis inside her, but also rubs his pubic area against her clitoris.

Module 16

Vibrating With Pleasure

It's a fact that most women masturbate. And many use a vibrator to help them. But the vibrator is not only a masturbatory tool. Many women who don't orgasm easily during intercourse or who enjoy prolonged, vigorous clitoral stimulation have turned to the vibrator for assistance.

It's fair to say that this has upset many men. They sometimes feel inadequate when faced with the idea that a machine can make their women happy, yet they cannot. But there's no reason that a sex toy should not be incorporated into sex play. If you understand and accept that most women cannot have orgasms from intercourse (as we discussed in the previous module), then perhaps you can think of the vibrator as simply one more technique for producing orgasm, along with oral sex and manual stimulation.

Many men enjoy taking a vibrator to bed with them. They enjoy using it on their partners, watching their partners use it, and having their partners use it during intercourse. Think of the vibrator as a sexual toy *for both of you,* and all of a sudden it's less of a threat and more of a joy. You can buy vibrators all over the place; in drug stores and small appliance stores, sex shops and catalogs (I've listed a few catalogs in the next module). You've probably seen these things in drug stores; you know, the box has a picture of an attractive woman using the vibrator on herself—rubbing her neck with it, that is.

Here are a few ways to use this toy:

- Use the vibrator while performing oral sex; the man can lick the woman's vaginal lips while the vibrator is placed on the clitoris. However, note that if she is not used to a vibrator, she may find her clitoris is much too sensitive to take direct stimulation; if so, the vibrator can be used around the clitoral area. You can experiment with different speeds (if it's a multi-speed model), or place some kind of thin material over the clitoris and then the vibrator on top.

- The man can lick the clitoris and vaginal lips while gently thrusting the vibrator in and out of her vagina. It's a great turn-on for many men to get close and watch as the vibrator "penetrates" their partners.

- Let the man watch while the woman uses the vibrator on herself. This is not only a very erotic experience, but he'll learn something, too.

- The man can enter the woman from behind—perhaps while both are lying on their sides—while she presses the vibrator to her clitoris or pubic area. This can create some interesting sensations for the man, too.

- The man can lie on his back, while the woman straddles him. He can take control of the vibrator, and use it on his partner's clitoris and vaginal lips while she slowly moves up and down on his penis.

- Lie together kissing and cuddling, while the man holds the vibrator; the woman should tell him what to do with it.

- Use the vibrator on the man; hold the tip to the penis until he orgasms. Run the vibrator from the top of the penis down to the testicles and back up again.

- While his partner is performing fellatio on him, the man can rub the vibrator around his genital area; on his testicles and perineum (the area between the testicles and anus), and on his inner thighs.

- The man can hold the vibrator to her clitoris while she performs oral sex on him.

- If the man is having trouble achieving an erection, hold the vibrator to the penis—it'll soon wake up!

Some couples feel that a vibrator somehow intrudes on the intimacy of the relationship. But don't think of the vibrator as a regular partner. Rather, consider the vibrator as an option, an addition to your creative sexual pleasure that you use now and again. It can also be used to "help out" occasionally. If the man doesn't want intercourse, he can use the vibrator on his partner instead of his erection. If the woman doesn't want intercourse during menstruation, she could use the vibrator to provide clitoral stimulation instead.

❊ ❊ The Pre-Orgasmic Woman and the Vibrator ❊ ❊

Vibrators can cause such intense sensations that some sex therapists recommend their use by women who have trouble reaching orgasm. The theory is that, if a woman suffers from great guilt or shame about sex, she may be unconsciously stopping her sexual organs from reaching orgasm; her subconscious simply won't allow it to happen. A vibrator, however, can blast through any such barriers. The sensations it creates can be so strong that it overwhelms any subconscious objections to orgasm. This can not only create an orgasm quickly, but it may allow the woman to eventually accept orgasms as a perfectly normal part of life, and finally to allow herself to have orgasms without the vibrator.

❊ ❊ Vibrator 101 ❊ ❊

Here's a good way for a man to start using a vibrator on his partner.

Don't go straight for the crotch the first time. Start by vibrating her neck, shoulders, and back, and only slowly move toward more erogenous zones. If the vibrator is a multispeed model, try the slowest speed when first getting acquainted.

With your partner on her back, slowly drag the vibrator around the front of her shoulders and breasts—be careful with the nipples, though, as the vibrator may be *too* stimulating. Move the vibrator slowly around her stomach, and down to the vaginal area.

Place the vibrator lightly on the lips of her vagina, and slide it up and down her vulva. After a few moments bring it close to the clitoris. If you are using one of the small, bullet-shaped vibrators, and if your partner is sufficiently lubricated, you might slide the vibrator into her vagina momentarily. (If you are using one of the larger, penis-like vibrators, you'll probably have to wait a while for that, until she's more aroused.)

When you use the vibrator directly on her clitoris, make sure you carefully observe her reaction. If necessary, reduce the pressure, and perhaps change the speed. Let her tell you where the vibrator feels best and the amount of pressure needed. (Every clitoris responds differently at different times, after all! There's no reason you should know exactly what this one likes, on this particular occasion.) She may want you to press with the vibrator only on the clitoris. Or perhaps she would like you to place the shaft of the vibrator on the clitoris, and press the tip down onto the vaginal lips.

Give your partner time to become accustomed to the new sensation. Some women are hesitant, and feel that it's not right to produce an orgasm in an *artificial* manner, that you should be using some body part to do that.

Let her take control if she wishes. While she uses the vibrator on herself, you can be using your hands, mouth, and penis. That way the route to orgasm isn't quite so artificial, and you *are* using part of your body to help her achieve orgasm. (Pay attention to what she's doing with the vibrator, though, so you'll learn what she likes for the next time you are given control.)

By the way, there's no need to work with just *one* vibrator. Some women really get into this battery-powered toy, and use multiple vibrators . . . it's easiest to do so with the help of a partner. One vibrator inside the vagina and one on the clitoris, for instance, or even one in the vagina and one on each nipple. As with all things sexual, let your imagination be your guide!

✱ ✱ Too Much of a Good Thing? ✱ ✱

Can you use a vibrator too much? Yes. There have been cases of women using vibrators so much that they become desensitized. They get used to the vibrations, and may eventually have to buy a heavy-duty, industrial-strength model to get the stimulation they need. These gadgets can also actually decrease a woman's ability to climax through intercourse or with manual and oral stimulation. Remember that the vibrator is just one sexual variation you can use; it shouldn't be a constant companion.

✱ ✱ Not Just for Her ✱ ✱

Many men enjoy using vibrators, so let him in on the fun, too. The woman can begin by giving him an oil massage, then lay him on his stomach and use the vibrator on his shoulders, neck, and back. With his body well oiled, you can press firmly onto his body with the vibrator and move it around in circular motions. Rub the vibrator over his buttocks and thighs, and run it along his inner thighs; you can tease him a little by pressing between his legs so it vibrates his testicles.

Then turn him over and continue rubbing the inner thighs. Don't rush to the genitals quite yet. Use it on his belly, chest, and arms. Then place it under the testicles, and against the perineum (the space between the testicles and the anus). Run it up the shaft, along the sensitive underside of the penis. But watch carefully; his penis, in particular the head of the penis, may be much too sensitive for direct stimulation with a vibrator and repeated use might desensitize the penis.

Of course the woman may enjoy this sort of vibrating massage, too, so take turns.

Sexual Position #14

Here's a nice position for use with a vibrator. You lie side by side, with the man entering from the rear. The woman can then use the vibrator on herself; on her clitoris and even on her vaginal lips as her partner thrusts. The man will be able to feel some unusual sensations, too, as the vibrations work their way through her body to his penis.

Module 17

Toys R Fun

*I*f you like playing with vibrators, have I got an idea for you! Take a look at some of the other sex toys on the market. You'll find all sorts of interesting bits and pieces designed to heighten sexual pleasure and bring new sensations—whether you are with a partner or alone.

But should you use sex toys? Many people feel that it's somehow dirty or unnatural. Some even feel threatened; if your partner needs a toy to become aroused, why does he or she need you? But toys don't have to be a replacement for a real relationship, they're just a bit of fun, another way to bring variety into your sex life. We're not suggesting that you pull out a sex toy every time you make love. But now and again doesn't do any harm (assuming you use the toy correctly!—read the instructions), and may feel good.

There are other reasons for sex toys, too. Masturbation is an obvious one; if your partner's away, and you need sexual relief, a sexual aid can help you. And how about long-distance sex? Many couples who are in the unfortunate position of spending a lot of time away from each other have sex over the phone. They call each other, chat for a little while, and then start "talking dirty." They start playing with themselves, telling each other what they are doing, and what they'd really like to do if they were together. Well, a couple of sex toys can really bring this experience alive. They can even "do it" long distance, telling each other exactly what to do and when. He can tell her when to place the vibrator on her clitoris, when to insert it into her vagina, how to thrust, and so on. He could use one of the many masturbation sheaths or penis-sucking machines (no, really!), to make the sensation of making love to his partner more realistic.

So approach this subject with an open mind. Try a couple of toys, and see if you enjoy it. If you live in or near a major city you may find that there's a well-stocked "toy store" you can visit to get a close look at what you are buying. If you *don't* have a local sex shop, then try some of the catalogs below:

- **Xandria Collection.** A very tasteful catalog, illustrated mainly with sketches. You won't feel sleazy using this one—they've gone out of their way to make buying sex toys fun, not smutty. 800-242-2823.
- **Good Vibrations.** This is run by the same women who run the Sexuality Library (see Module 29). It's a company dedicated to making buying sex toys a pleasant, not tacky, experience. 800-289-8423 or 415-974-8990.
- **Eve's Garden.** A catalog with sexual toys and erotica of interest to women. 800-848-3837.
- **Adam & Eve.** A fairly explicit catalog with lots of pictures of videos and sex toys. 800-765-2326.
- **Voyages.** Another glossy catalog, but with more focus on sex toys than Adam & Eve. 415-863-4822.
- **Leisure Time Products.** A *very* explicit catalog with many videos and a few pages of toys and clothing. 800-874-8960.

There are other companies selling sex toys, of course. You can find more catalogs advertised in men's and erotic magazines. Be warned that these catalogs can be extremely explicit. They vary from Xandria's tasteful restraint to Leisure Time Products' extremely candid catalog. Still, we're talking about sex here; if you plan to call for these catalogs you may be surprised by what you find, but probably not shocked.

❀ ❀ Pick Your Plaything ❀ ❀

Let's see what you might want to play with.

- **Vibrators.** We discussed vibrators in Module 16. You'll find all kinds, from the small white ones you find in drug stores that look nothing like a penis, to giant phalluses with multiple direction motion and vibrating; some churn around in circles, or pump up or down. You'll find all sorts of weird and wonderful shapes, sizes, and textures.
- **G-spot Vibrators.** These are specially curved vibrators. The last third or quarter of the vibrator curves to one side, the idea being that it's ideally shaped to stimulate the G spot.

- **Clitoral Vibrators.** These are held onto the woman with thin straps that run around her legs and hips. There are a few varieties, such as the Venus Butterfly (which rests against the vagina and clitoris and vibrates), and the Stingray (which also has a vibrating tail designed for insertion into the anus). Some women like to wear these during the day, a great way to make work a little more interesting. Some of these vibrators are small enough to be worn during intercourse.

- **Vibrators with Attachments.** Some vibrators come with special attachments, the idea being that while vibrating inside the vagina it can also stimulate the clitoris. You might have a bunny's ears fluttering around your clitoris, a beaver's tongue, a fish's fins, or an elephant's trunk! These vibrators are often designed to look like something out of an oriental sex-toy store, with faces molded into the tip of the vibrator. In fact, many of these come from Japan.

- **Ben-Wa Balls.** These are metal or plastic balls that are placed in the vagina; as the woman moves, a small heavy ball inside moves around, causing the Ben-Wa balls to vibrate.

- **Vibrating Eggs.** Similar to Ben-Wa balls, only with electrically controlled vibrations. A variety of "eggs" and other types that can be put into the vagina and vibrated. One kind is even remote controlled—no wires. This could be a great accessory for when she acts as his concubine for the day! (See Module 36.)

- **Bondage Tethers.** If you like tying down your lover, but haven't yet found anything suitable, you can buy special straps that hold without chafing. You can buy blindfolds, too, shackles, harnesses . . . anything you can imagine.

- **Penis Sleeves.** These are textured sleeves that fit over the penis, the intention being to bring new sensations to the woman during intercourse.

- **Chinese Love Beads.** These are small beads on a string, with a ring at one end. They are inserted into the anus before or during intercourse . . . then, at the point of orgasm, pulled out, adding an unusual sensation to orgasm that can heighten the pleasure.

- **Masturbation Sheaths.** These vary from clear inflatable sheaths to imitation vaginas!

- **Penis-Sucking Machines.** The male equivalent of the vibrator; he slips his penis into a sheath which then vibrates or sucks in some way.

- **Penis Vibrators.** Special rings fit around the base of the penis. They vibrate, bringing pleasure to the man, and vibrate the clitoris during intercourse.

- **Breast Stimulation Tools.** From large cones that slip over the entire breast and suck, to small tubes that are placed over the nipples and suck.

- **Cockstraps.** These slip around the penis and testicles. They help the man maintain his erection for longer periods.
- **Scrotum Straps.** If you put your fingers around the scrotum at the point that it joins the body, such that the testicles are below the ring made by your fingers, you'll find that you can control orgasm (we looked at this *scrotal tug* in Module 11); as long as you are holding the testicles like this, you won't come. You can get special straps that can do the holding for you, which can be released quickly when you are ready for an orgasm.
- **Potions and Lotions.** All sorts of interesting lotions are available; pheromones (designed to turn on your partner . . . or help you find a partner); all sorts of lubricants; Tantric foot creams, massage oils; lotions that warm the skin, and taste good when licked off; creams designed to delay ejaculation; oral-sex gel (feels good being rubbed onto his penis, tastes good when sucked off).
- **Sex Games.** You'll find a variety of card, book, and board games . . . even a sexual dart game. A nice way to break down inhibitions and to introduce variety into your lovemaking. You can buy games designed for couples, or for small groups if you're into that.
- **Audio Erotica.** The new thing in erotica is *listening* to it. You can buy tapes and CDs with the sounds of passionate lovemaking. Not quite as exciting as watching it for most people, but some really get turned on by listening.

I've only described some of the more common toys you'll find. Take a look at a few catalogs, and you'll be amazed at the sexual ingenuity that has gone into some of this stuff! How about a bath sponge that vibrates as you rub it over your body (and between your legs) while lying in the bath? Or a five-speed imitation tongue from Japan, which can be used on its own, or even attached to a penis so it licks her clitoris while the man is inside her? Or a saddle with a phallus on the seat?

There's an entire industry dedicated to finding new and strange ways to turn you on . . . mechanically. In the future you can expect to see virtual reality sex toys that are connected to computers—as you view sexual images and hear the sounds of sex, the toys will stimulate your body at the correct time and in the correct way. A man might have a virtual blow job—he'll see a woman sucking him, hear the sounds of the sucking . . . and feel her doing it at the same time. The same for a woman; she'll see the man, feel him as he licks her, and feel him as he moves up and enters her. All thanks to the wonders of the PC revolution! There's even a magazine dedicated to the subject: *Future Sex.* Much of this technology already exists, it just hasn't been commercialized yet. It will be. (We just hope people don't forget that there's nothing quite like the real thing.)

Sexual Position #15

This position is a sort of transitory position; the man won't be doing any prolonged thrusting with this, and the woman's arms may tire after a while. Still, she can use her arms and legs to move around on his penis, and he can use his hands and mouth on her nipples and breasts.

The easiest way to try this position is to start with the oceanic position that we looked at in Module 9—the woman lies on her back, and the man kneels between her legs. He puts his hands under her buttocks, lifts her, and enters her. Then, as he moves his hands behind her back and lifts, she raises herself up on her arms.

Module 18

Oral Sex: Cunnilingus

As you almost certainly know, oral sex does *not* mean talking about it. Oral sex is a widely practiced sexual act in which the mouth does most of the work, though just a few years ago it was labeled a perversion. Actually it's still illegal in some states, though you won't often hear of anyone getting locked up for it. To be precise, oral sex between members of the opposite sex is illegal in Alabama, Arizona, Florida, Georgia, Idaho, Louisiana, Michigan, Minnesota, Mississippi, North Carolina, Rhode Island, South Carolina, Utah, and Virginia. If you live in one of these states you have two options; you can skip to another module, or you can do as most other sexually active people do in your state, ignore these laws.

It's actually our lawmakers who are out of step. Oral sex has undoubtedly been around for thousands of years. It's mentioned in the *Kama Sutra* (written perhaps as many as 2,000 years ago) and in Tantric writings, and shown on ancient Peruvian pottery. It appears to be common to most, perhaps all, cultures. People apparently are born with an innate desire to use their mouths sexually, which is not surprising when you consider that most mammals indulge in a little oral sex now and again, too. (Or a lot. Horses sometimes use oral sex for hours on end.)

Just how widely is it practiced? We can safely say that these days *most* sexually active people indulge in oral sex at least now and again, as a form of foreplay or sometimes in place of intercourse. And, according to social psychologists

Carol Tavris, Ph.D., and Susan Sadd, Ph.D. (commenting on their analysis of a survey published in *Redbook* in the 1970s), women who have oral sex most often and enjoy it the most "are those who are most likely to say their sex lives and their marriages are excellent." It's not only common, it's good for you, too.

Of course there are two forms of oral sex: the use of the mouth to stimulate the woman's clitoris and vagina (cunnilingus), and the use of the mouth to stimulate the man's penis and testicles (fellatio). In the old-fashioned spirit of allowing the ladies to go first, we're going to start this look at oral sex with cunnilingus, and in the next module take a look at fellatio. Before we get started, though, here's a quick self-test for you both, designed to teach you about your feelings related to oral sex, to see if you are both "in sync" with your desires.

	Questions for Him	**Questions for Her**
	Have you ever performed cunnilingus?	Have you ever performed fellatio?
Yes		
No		
	If no, would you like to?	If no, would you like to?
Yes		
No		
	If you *have* performed cunnilingus, why do you/did you do so?	If you *have* performed fellatio, why do you/did you do so?
To arouse my lover		
To bring my partner to orgasm		
To arouse us both		
Primarily to arouse myself		
Because my partner wants it		

	If you *have* performed cunnilingus, which of these statements best describe your feelings?	If you *have* performed fellatio which of these statements best describe your feelings?
It gives me great pleasure		
It heightens my own arousal		
I enjoy giving my partner pleasure		
I enjoy giving oral sex, but don't want my partner to orgasm that way		
I prefer oral sex only as foreplay		
I like it when we move on to mutual oral sex (69), which may or may not lead to orgasm for one or both of us		
I don't enjoy it, but do it for his/her pleasure		
I don't like the way women's/men's genitals look		
I don't like the way women's/men's genitals smell		
It disgusts me		

Oral Sex: Cunnilingus

	Have you ever been the recipient of oral sex?	Have you ever been the recipient of oral sex?
Yes		
No		
	If no, would you like to?	If no, would you like to?
Yes		
No		
	If you've received oral sex, how does it usually feel to you?	If you've received oral sex, how does it usually feel to you?
Fantastic		
Highly stimulating		
Fairly stimulating		
Pleasant		
Makes me anxious		
Unpleasant—I really don't like it!		
	In an average month, how often do you get oral sex?	In an average month, how often do you get oral sex?
I get it less than once a month		
Once or twice		
3 to 5 times		
5 to 10 times		
More than ten times		
	How often would you like to?	How often would you like to?
Once or twice		
3 to 5 times		

	In an average month, how often do you perform cunnilingus?	In an average month, how often do you perform fellatio?
5 to 10 times		
More than ten times		
Once or twice		
3 to 5 times		
5 to 10 times		
More than ten times		
	How often would you like to?	How often would you like to?
Once or twice		
3 to 5 times		
5 to 10 times		
More than ten times		
	How often do you orgasm from fellatio?	How often do you orgasm from cunnilingus?
Always		
Frequently		
Half the time		
Never		
	How often would you like to?	How often would you like to?
Always		
Frequently		
Half the time		
Never		

If you disagree about oral sex, it's a good idea to talk about it—but not immediately before, during, or after sex. Discuss it during a calm, nonsexual moment, and allow enough time to talk it all out. Don't get angry. Just

Oral Sex: Cunnilingus

because, for instance, the woman finds fellatio distasteful, doesn't mean there's something wrong with her. Sex is all about personal taste, and what's right for you may be wrong for someone else. The following information (**The Aesthetics of Oral Sex**) may help. Also, you may each want to make a few promises—the man may agree not to come in his partner's mouth, to warn her before he ejaculates. (Yes, yes, we know the old joke, the world's biggest lies: *The check's in the mail, I won't come in your mouth,* and so on. If you say you won't, you'd better mean it.) If the woman is concerned about choking (men have a tendency to get carried away and thrust too hard), you can agree on a position in which the woman has control—and she can grasp the shaft of the penis with her hand to stop the whole thing going in! You might also agree to make sure the lights are out when you have oral sex—this may help a shy partner.

The woman may agree to a "swap," that she'll fellate him if he promises to reciprocate equally, or maybe she'll sell him so many "blow jobs" in return for some other sexual act she enjoys. Or perhaps you can do a swap based on two of the most common sexual "wants." Men often want more oral sex. Women often want more cuddling. How about a 6:1 swap, for instance: Six minutes of cuddling equals 1 minute of oral sex.

Use your imagination, and you may be able to get closer to satisfying both partners in this area. There are some people who will simply never enjoy oral sex, though, and if your partner happens to be one of these people there's little you can do about it. You shouldn't insist that your partner carry out a sexual act that he or she finds unpleasant. Conflict over oral sex is one of the most common problems between partners, and the occasional divorce has been based on this problem.

By the way, if you don't enjoy performing oral sex, but agree to do so because your partner really wants it, do it without making it look like you really hate it. There's nothing less exciting than having someone perform oral sex with a look of revulsion on his or her face!

❃ ❃ The Aesthetics of Oral Sex ❃ ❃

Let's be blunt; there are certain taste and odor issues involved here! Many people are a little wary—okay, more than a little wary in many cases—of the taste or odor of their partner's genitals. Many women are happy to perform fellatio, up to a point. Most women do not like the idea of having a man ejaculating into their mouths. Many men find the musky taste and smell of their partner's genitals slightly off-putting. And if you've used a lubricated condom, or spermicidal jelly or cream, before performing cunnilingus, the taste can be quite unpleasant. So, here are a few tips for oral sex:

- It (almost) goes without saying that you should both be very clean. Wash with warm soapy water beforehand.
- Keep lubricated condoms, lubricants, jellies, creams, and whatever, away from the vagina until *after* you've finished with oral sex! Or buy the flavored versions.
- Understand that there's nothing perilous in a man's ejaculate. It's merely protein, fructose, minerals, and water (sounds almost appetizing when you put it like that!), and swallowing it can do no harm. (It's even slightly nutritious, though claims many women have heard that it will smooth facial wrinkles, add sheen to the hair, firm sagging breasts, make you look ten years younger, or cure world hunger are, unfortunately, without basis in fact.)
- Vaginal fluids, too, are innocuous. They are a saliva-like fluid. The vagina generally has fewer bacteria than the mouth!
- Believe it or not, a taste for the musky odor of the vagina is one that many men can acquire. Some men report that breathing the odor in deeply helps them get over their initial uneasiness, and many eventually find the odor sexually exciting. However, most men want their women's genitals to be freshly washed and odor free.
- The Chinese once believed that cunnilingus was a way for the man to procure *yin* essence from the woman (to complement the male's inherent *yang* essence), of which women apparently have an inexhaustible supply. So cunnilingus is actually good for you. (Assuming you believe this *yin-yang* stuff, of course.)

✻ ✻ A Kiss on the Lips—Cunnilingus ✻ ✻

Cunnilingus is not, to paraphrase a schoolboy joke, an Irish airline. Rather, it's the term used to describe the stimulation of a woman's genitals with the mouth and tongue. It's a very intimate form of sexual contact—most men in our studies (eighty-seven percent) said that they will perform cunnilingus on a woman only if they feel emotionally secure with her. There has to be some form of relationship closer than a one-night stand or even a casual affair before they're prepared to get that physically close. (Many men also state that they will only perform cunnilingus on a woman who is in just the right shape—while they may be prepared to have intercourse with a heavy woman, for instance, they may be unwilling to perform cunnilingus on her. Another reason for a woman to read Modules 2 and 3.)

We also found that ninety percent of young men enjoy performing cunnilingus, and this seems to be borne out by Shere Hite's studies. (Older men, fifty-eight and over, are less likely to find pleasure in cunnilingus. We found that only twenty percent of these men said they enjoyed it.) Men who enjoyed it said they find that not only does the woman like what they are doing, but that they themselves become more sexually excited, too. Here's a typical comment: "When I watch my lover respond to oral sex with thrusts and twitches of her pelvis, when I hear her moans, I'm totally lost in the moment." Cunnilingus can be *extremely* exciting for many women, and in turn a man witnessing the intensity of his lover's pleasure—and knowing that what *he's* doing is responsible—is likely to get even more turned on himself.

There are other reasons to perform cunnilingus, too. There's the selfish reason, cited by many younger men, that if they perform cunnilingus the woman may reciprocate; that is, she is more likely to perform fellatio (selfish, perhaps, but probably correct). And then there's a reason cited by some older men—that cunnilingus provides a way to increase a woman's arousal when the man is unable to maintain an erection. And oral sex is an excellent way to start the vagina's natural lubrication flowing. Cunnilingus is often used for foreplay—only about one third of men actually bring their partners to orgasm through the use of their mouths (it's often rather tiring, though practice will strengthen your tongue).

Cunnilingus is performed by gently mouthing and tonguing the vaginal area. You can use a variety of techniques: licking the vaginal lips and around the clitoris, sucking and licking very gently on the clitoris, licking up and down the vaginal opening, and inserting the tongue into the vagina.

There are many ways that the man can position himself so that he can reach the vagina with his mouth. She may lie on her back with her legs apart while he kneels before her, between her legs. He may kneel next to her, with his feet toward her head and his head between her legs. One particularly exciting position is for the man to lie on his back while the woman kneels over him. As he uses his mouth he can also reach up to squeeze and caress her breasts, or reach behind her and caress her buttocks. Or she may kneel and rest on her elbows, while the man licks her vagina from behind. (This can be used as an interesting little "surprise" cunnilingus, by the way; you may be surprised at your partner's response if, as she kneels expecting you to insert your penis, you begin licking her instead). The woman may stand, with the man kneeling before her . . . use your imagination, and find whatever position is comfortable!

Use a variety of motions with your tongue and lips, on the clitoris, the labia, the vagina itself, the perineum (which I'll explain in a moment) and even the thighs and buttocks. Don't think you have to use just one stroke or technique—vary them unless the woman asks you to continue with a particu-

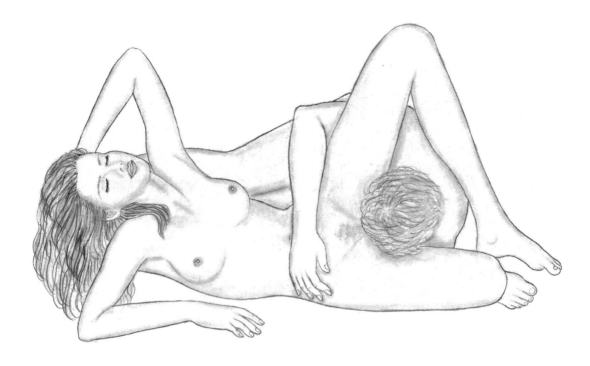

lar method. By the way, there's an important advantage to using a variety of motions; you'll be able to last longer before you get too tired to continue.

✳ ✳ Don't Dive Right In ✳ ✳

It's a good idea to start *around* the vagina and not plunge right in. Kiss and nibble her belly and her thighs, for instance, or start even further away, by sucking her breasts and nipples, and then move down. Move gradually to the vaginal area, kissing and licking around the pubic mound. It's often exciting if the woman is still wearing panties when you begin; you can lick around the edge of the panties, even suck the vaginal area through the panties, then eventually pull them to one side to reveal the vagina and clitoris.

Don't forget the perineum, either. This is an extremely sensitive area of her body; it's the area between the vagina and the anus. She'll have to open her legs quite wide to allow you to reach it (so in some positions you won't be able to get there). Having the perineum licked is a great turn-on for many women.

✳ ✳ The Labia and Vagina ✳ ✳

Lick up and down the outer vaginal lips (the labia), on the lips themselves and between them. Try sucking the lips very gently into your mouth. And insert your tongue into the vagina; try quick shallow motions, deep, slow insertions, and so on. Be careful with your teeth though; your partner won't appreciate being bitten in this sensitive area!

✶ ✶ The Clitoris ✶ ✶

Remember that the clitoris is very sensitive, so it normally requires fairly gentle stimulation (though let your partner's responses be your guide). And because it is so sensitive, you may want to leave it until last, until your partner has already become quite aroused by your licking and sucking elsewhere in the vaginal area.

You may need to use your fingers to part the vaginal lips so you can find the clitoris (see Module 8 for an illustration showing the clitoris' position). In some cases you can just use your tongue to do so. Stroke your tongue up and down over the shaft and head of the clitoris. Try very light strokes of the tongue on the head of the clitoris, and flicking from side to side with your tongue across the shaft of the clitoris. Try gently sucking the clitoris, too. The man should ask his partner what feels good—and the woman should not be afraid to tell him. While women often feel that their man "should just know what's good," this is a little unfair; each woman is different, and what may have worked for a man's earlier partners may do nothing for a current partner.

✶ ✶ Don't Forget the Rest of the Body ✶ ✶

Don't ignore the rest of her body while you are dispensing oral pleasure. Depending on the position you are using, you can caress her buttocks, breasts, belly, the backs of her legs, and so on. Many women enjoy having their inner thighs nibbled and kissed, too, and may want to use their own hands for further stimulation—to rub and squeeze the breasts and nipples, for instance, or their inner thighs.

You may want to insert one or two fingers into the vagina while you lick around her vagina, too. You can use the fingers to stimulate the G spot (which we'll talk about more in Module 28), or simply stroke inside the vagina. And many women will love having a vibrator inserted into the vagina during cunnilingus, too (see Modules 16 and 17 for information about such toys).

Sexual Position #16

You saw one possible cunnilingus position earlier in this chapter; well, here's another, more unusual one. The man holds his partner's legs up, revealing her vagina erotically framed by her buttocks. After oral sex he might keep her in this position, kneel in front of her and place her legs over his shoulders, and insert his penis.

Oral Sex: Cunnilingus

Oral Sex: Fellatio

A h, now for the man's turn. Fellatio, more commonly known as a *blow job* (or *smoking, suck the sugar stick, serve head, and the French way,* in some places), consists of the woman using her mouth to stimulate the man's penis. (If you haven't read Module 18 yet, go back for more background information about oral sex.)

✂ ✂ Learning Fellatio ✂ ✂

An inexperienced woman may be introduced to fellatio slowly, by a little demonstration using fingers. The man takes the woman's middle finger and demonstrates how he enjoys having his penis caressed and sucked using his own mouth and hands. Then you swap; the woman now takes the man's middle finger and copies the techniques she just saw. (Actually sucking on each other's fingers in this manner is sensual in its own right.) She moves her mouth from the tip to the base, with a gentle sucking motion, and moves her tongue around or along the shaft of the finger. After a few minutes of practice, the man replaces his finger with his penis, and uses words of encouragement to tell her how good she makes him feel.

In some cases a woman may need an even simpler introduction. If a woman finds the mere idea of getting her partner's penis anywhere near her mouth hard to consider, she might be introduced slowly by encouraging her to kiss

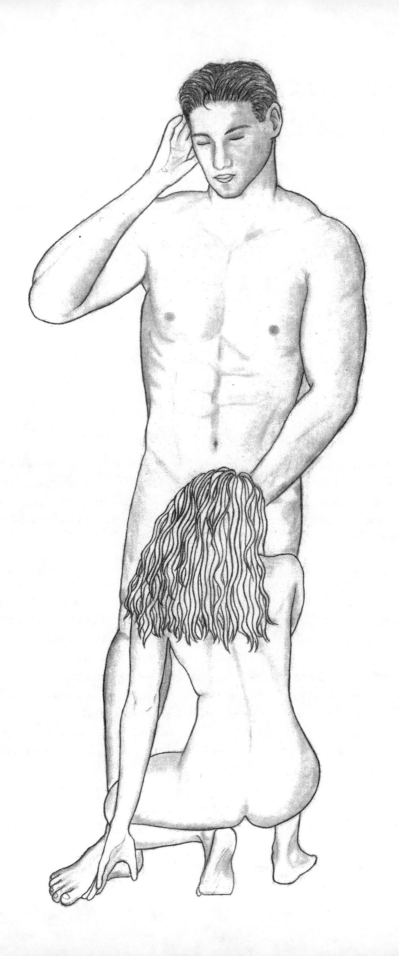

and nibble the man's belly and thighs, and later to simply kiss the shaft of the penis. It may take several lovemaking sessions for the woman to become fully comfortable with taking the penis into her mouth, but it's better to take your time than rush her.

What positions are suitable for fellatio? There are many; he may lie on his back with the woman between his knees. He may stand while she kneels before him. She may lie to one side of him, with her feet near his head (this position has the added attraction of allowing the man to caress her buttocks and vagina as she sucks him, or even to lean over and nibble her thighs and buttocks—it's also simple to move from simple fellatio to 69 from this position).

However, not all positions are equal. Ideally the woman needs to be able to get to the underside of the penis, in which case she needs to be between his legs, facing "up." This position allows her to "play the jade flute," as the Chinese used to call it; she holds his penis like a musical instrument, with her thumb underneath and fingers on top, and sucks the tip of the penis.

By the way, men's responses to oral stimulation of the glans—the tip of the penis—vary greatly. Most find it quite wonderful, while others won't allow it. In particular many uncircumcised men prefer movement of the foreskin over the glans, rather than direct stimulation of the glans.

✻✻ Try This . . . ✻✻

Here's an example of how a woman might approach fellatio.

Begin by caressing the penis and testicles with gentle strokes, along the shaft of the penis and over the head, and gently suck the head, like a baby sucking a mother's nipple. If you can manage to do so, breathe through your nose while sucking, so you don't have to stop to breathe. You'll find that your saliva production is stimulated, providing lubrication to the penis. And don't forget to swallow your own saliva . . . you'll find it builds up quickly.

Lick up and down the penis, on each side and on the underside, which is very sensitive. Try quick, light flicks along and across the underside, too. Gently kiss and nibble the sides of the penis, while you hold the tip of the penis in your hand.

Then take the penis into your mouth, and use a variety of motions; you might clasp the penis between your lips very lightly, and take as much into your mouth as possible, until the tip touches the back of your mouth (though be careful not to gag). You might suck hard, and move your mouth back up the shaft, increasing the sucking as you reach the head and moving the tongue around the head. However, be careful with your teeth; keep them to yourself! They won't feel good to your partner if they touch the penis, so do your best to cover your teeth with your lips.

Try licking the head of his penis, with a relaxed, wide tongue motion, moving

Oral Sex: Fellatio

your tongue around and around the head, getting it quite wet as you do so; then suck gently on it. And don't forget the testicles and inner thighs. Suck and lick the testicles, and nibble on his thighs at the point at which his testicles join his body. When you are using your mouth on his penis, hold and very gently squeeze his testicles, rub his thighs, and, depending on the position, squeeze his buttocks.

As you suck, you can use your hand to "masturbate" him, too, using up and down strokes on the penis. And if you can trust your partner not to get carried away and thrust too deeply, you might also want to lie on your side and let him gently thrust into your mouth. If you plan to let him come in your mouth, this may be a nice way to do it. Once he's come, let him stay in your mouth a few moments, and softly suck as he loses his erection.

✄ ✄ Where Are You Going to Come? ✄ ✄

Most men are excited by the idea of coming in their partner's mouths. Perhaps it's the idea of complete sexual abandon, or simply that they feel if they get that aroused, they might as well go all the way—to suddenly stop and change position or technique can be frustrating. Unfortunately, some women *don't* like having a man come in their mouth.

If the woman simply won't, then what's to do? She might remove her mouth at the last moment, and continue with her hand until he ejaculates. Or perhaps quickly change position and allow him to thrust between her breasts. Or he might quickly enter her vagina. Perhaps the best situation is if the man can tell his partner when he's about to come, so she can immediately withdraw the penis and finish with her hand. Using this method there is little or no interruption in "flow." Remember, though, if you come without warning her, it may be the last time your penis will get anywhere near her mouth.

Ideally the woman will eventually get used to the idea of taking it in her mouth. She may be willing to give it a try, especially for a man she is very close to. And consider that some women enjoy having a man come in their mouths—they find both the taste and experience sexually exciting. But on the other hand, she may never agree. The man shouldn't make this a sore point in the relationship, though; just accept that people's sexual tastes vary greatly.

✄ ✄ How About Soixante-Neuf? ✄ ✄

The number sixty-nine—*soixante-neuf* in French—has been cursed (or blessed, perhaps, depending on your point of view). It's impossible for most adults in the western world to see that number without thinking of oral sex! One American newspaper editor even edited a story about a sixty-nine-car pileup,

The Best Sex of Your Life

reporting (to avoid using this most "obscene" of numbers), that there were *seventy* cars involved in the pileup. (Quickly, how many professional football players can you name who have the number sixty-nine on their jerseys?)

Sixty-nine (sometimes known as *loop-de-loop or flip flop*) actually refers to a variety of positions, in which the only common theme is that the couple is performing oral sex on each other. The man may be lying on his back, with the woman on top, her mouth on his penis and his mouth on her clitoris and vagina. Or maybe he's on top. Or maybe they are side by side, with heads resting on the partner's thigh. The really daring might even try standing up, with the man holding the woman around the torso and the woman head down. (Of course you have to have just the right combination of strong man, slight woman, and trust. It doesn't matter, take your pick.)

Oral Sex: Fellatio

The idea of sixty-nine is extremely erotic, though the reality is often not quite so. The problem is that it's difficult for both to "give their all" at the same time. As any man will tell you, it's very hard to concentrate on *technique* of any kind when someone's sucking your penis! (Which is why being fellated while driving isn't a good idea, by the way.)

Still, mutual oral sex can be very exciting and intimate, if you treat it a little differently. Don't go into it expecting that both partners will do their best. It's often better if one partner is the "primary" partner, the one doing most of the work, while the other is allowed to lie back and enjoy it much of the time, bringing his or her mouth into play only when the feeling strikes. Sixty-nine can be very pleasurable when it's an extension of straight cunnilingus or fellatio —the man, for instance, begins by kissing and licking his partner's vagina and clitoris, then, after a while, brings his body around so his penis is now in reach of his partner's mouth. She may wish to finish oral sex to orgasm, or she may want to gently suck on the head of his penis as he continues his work.

Incidentally, take a look again at Module 11. You'll find a description of the "scrotal tug," a method that can be used to delay orgasm. It's a great little accessory to fellatio, as the woman can use it to hold him back as long as she wants, and release him at will to experience an explosive orgasm.

Sexual Position #17

Have you ever tried this position? Look closely and you'll see that the woman's legs are between the man's legs, not the other way round as is normal. You'll have to start using the normal missionary position—the man between the woman's legs—but once his penis is in her vagina she closes her legs and he places his either side of hers. It provides an unusual sensation, a delicious tightness on the penis and perhaps more clitoral stimulation, as the man tends to "ride higher" with his pelvis pressed against her pubic area.

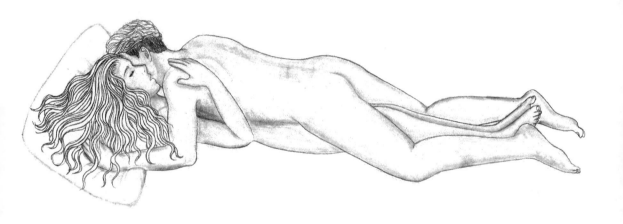

Module 20

The Sexual Vacation

When you are trying to break a habit, it's often useful to think about the conditions related to the habit. For instance, smokers often find that there are certain times of the day and activities that lead to smoking; they may sit down mid-morning with a cup of coffee and a cigarette, for instance, or have a beer in the evening . . . and a cigarette. Well, if you are determined to break a habit, you may want to start by changing the related conditions. *Don't* have a coffee mid-morning, *don't* have a beer in the evening, and so on.

The habit you want to break right now is boring sex. What conditions are associated with boring sex? Many couples (okay, most), get into a sexual routine. They only have sex in the evening, after watching television, they only have sex in their own bed, they may only have sex on a particular day—Saturday night, for instance. Most couples are, quite understandably, preoccupied with the chores of everyday life. They drag themselves home from work, make dinner, help the kids with homework, bathe the kids, get them off to bed, and so on. Then there's time to relax . . . usually watching television. By the time they've calmed down and feel a little more human, it's time for bed—they have to be up early in the morning and repeat the day's routine, after all—so there's not much time for sex. "Sex," in fact, is likely to be nothing more than a quick kiss goodnight. If the couple *does* have sex, it's likely to be a "quickie." (Even a quickie late at night is better than nothing, of course. As science-fiction author Robert Heinlein said, "It's better to copulate than never.")

Well, how about changing one of those conditions, and seeing what happens. Take a sexual vacation. You may have heard friends make euphemistic comments about a recent vacation, with a slight chuckle or gleam in their eyes. Comments such as "it was like a second honeymoon," or "it did her good . . . believe me, she was a different woman," or perhaps something more blatant. And it's true that vacations really *do* lead to good sex. Getting away from the same old routine, from work, home, the kids even, allows couples to relax and spend more time on sex.

But you don't need to fly to the Caribbean to take a sexual vacation. Why not take a vacation close to home?

- Find someone to look after the kids, and check into a hotel for an evening. Spend time in the restaurant, relaxing in the hot tub, watching an adult movie in your room. And *don't* rush to get up in the morning. We can almost guarantee that you'll remember the sex for a long time.
- If a friend asks you to house sit, jump at the offer. Simply being in a different environment can be enough to shake the cobwebs loose.
- Take a trip into the mountains or to the beach. Don't rush around too much, just spend time taking a romantic walk in the woods or on the beach, then go back to your hotel and work some magic. Or make love where you happen to be when the feeling takes you. (Be careful, though, and take the advice of British actress Evelyn Laye: "Sex, unlike justice, should not be seen to be done." Unfortunately sex outdoors is illegal in most places).
- When was the last time you made love in a tent? Take that trip to the mountains or the beach, but stay at a camp site. One of the nice things about camping is that there's no television to distract you. The evenings are long and relaxed . . . what else is there to do but play?
- If you can't afford the time and money to go away for the weekend, you can still vacation at home. Send the kids to stay with friends or family, then do something unusual. Take a walk in the local park at dusk, and eat a light meal at a favorite restaurant. Then go home, but make sure the television remains *off!* Turn off the ringer on the telephone, then take a leisurely shower or warm bath together.

Whatever form of vacation you take, here are a few guidelines:

- Set aside time for each other; you can't rush this, the whole idea is to take things slowly.
- You must stop thinking about your daily worries; forget about work, financial problems, the kids. You want to refocus on each other, not on the outside world.
- Do something different. Break the normal routines. That's easy to do if

you've gone away for a vacation, but it's also essential if you are taking a sexual vacation at home.

- Don't feel that you have to rush the sex, that you must jump straight into it. Take it slowly. Remember, you've set aside the time, so there's no hurry.
- Turn off the television (unless there's something erotic playing). Karl Marx may have felt that religion was the opiate of the masses, but that's because television hadn't been invented back then. It's easy to get lured into watching a show (the TV companies know how to do that, they've had half a century of practice), and lose the feeling of intimacy with your partner that you are trying to create.

✻ ✻ The Marital Rendezvous ✻ ✻

Here's a variation on the theme: Schedule a marital rendezvous. Think of this as a very quick vacation. The idea is not to set aside a whole day or weekend for the vacation. Perhaps right now you don't have time for that. But you can schedule an evening (or a morning, or afternoon, or whatever time you want) for a sexual rendezvous.

It's sometimes a good idea to set a specific date and time for such an event. Mark it on the calendar. That's not to say that you can't have sex at other times, before the rendezvous, of course. But at least once it's set it should be regarded as a promise to each other, to be broken only by accident or sickness. Scheduling a rendezvous makes sure that you *will* fit sex into your busy schedule. If you always seem too busy for sex, if sex always seems to come last, you may find that scheduling makes it easier to put it at the top of the "To Do" list.

Some people don't like the idea of scheduling sex this way. They say it just doesn't seem right. After all, they would claim, sex should be spontaneous. Sure, sex should be spontaneous, *and* it should be planned, *and* it should be regular, *and* it should be often, *and* it should be fun. Planning it now and again doesn't mean it can't be spontaneous, too; there's no rule that you can't have sex until the scheduled day. But scheduling sex has the advantage of making room in your busy lives for sex. It also has the added advantage of *anticipation.* Many couples enjoy the anticipation that comes from knowing that *tonight's the night!* Remember that in earlier modules we talked about how women regard arousal as something that can go on for hours, before any sexual contact has been made? That simply talking with each other can be part of arousal? Well, imagine just how aroused you both will become knowing that you'll be making love tonight.

You can add to the feeling of sexual anticipation, too. Before you leave home in the morning talk about what you are going to do that evening. Spend a few minutes making flirtatious or sensual phone calls to your partner at work. Agree to meet at a hotel—maybe one of those hotels where people go for only one reason, and the rooms are rented by the hour! Bring along some cheese, crackers, fresh fruit, a couple of glasses, and a bottle of juice, wine, or champagne. (Sip on the drink before sex, and finish it after! Don't drink too much or you won't enjoy what you are there for!)

If you still can't get used to the idea of scheduling sex, try it with something else. A walk in the park, for instance, or a visit to the health club where you can have a gentle workout and a long soak in the hot tub. Schedule a massage, or a jog together. Then, when you've finished, make love. (If you can link sex to other activities, you'll soon be like Pavlov's dogs, salivating every time you think of your scheduled walk or workout.) You didn't schedule sex, but there's no reason you shouldn't include it. If the scheduled activity is pleasant, out of the ordinary, and allows sufficient time afterward for a little physical closeness, then why not?

Sexual Position #18

Here's an interesting position for tonight. The woman starts with her legs apart, while the man enters her from behind. You may find it easier if the woman is kneeling when you start, and then lies down after the man has entered her. She can then close her legs. This provides a nice snug fit for the penis.

Some women find this position very stimulating, because the penis angles down toward the G spot on the front wall of the vagina (see Module 28). The man can hold onto the woman's arms or shoulders, or even lean forward and hold onto the headboard. He may also alternate this position with one in which he brings his legs forward, a knee on each side of her thighs, and kneels up. This provides him with a very exciting view, in which he sees his partner's buttocks and can watch his penis as it thrusts into her vagina. He can also caress her buttocks from this position. (He'll have to be reasonably limber for this kneeling position, as the legs are necessarily stretched wide apart. It's similar to a yoga position, though more fun!)

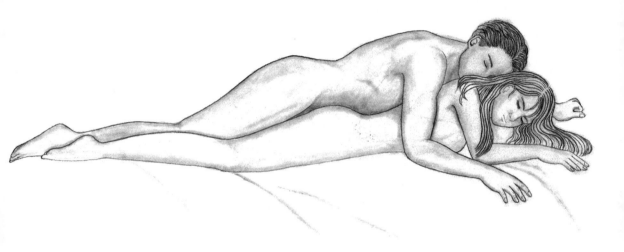

Module 21

Mirror, Mirror, on the Wall

Men know all about watching. They are very visual creatures, turned on by the sight of an attractive woman, a little bit of skin, the curve of a breast under a sweater . . . it often doesn't take much. (Arabic cultures know this, which is why they keep their women completely covered. Of course, the more of a woman that is customarily covered, the slighter the view that is required to excite a man. As the Victorians knew, the sight of an ankle could be more than a man could bear.)

Viewing flesh is not solely a male pleasure. Most women enjoy it, too. *Playgirl's* readers are not *all* homosexual men, by any means. So in some ways it seems a little unfair that it's often easier for men to watch what's going on during sex than for a woman. A number of positions have the delightful advantage of providing a great vantage point. When a couple has sex "doggie style," for instance, the man gets to see a view that the woman can only imagine, a highly erotic view of his penis thrusting into her. A number of "man on top" positions also allow the man to sit up and watch as he moves in and out of her. The woman, if she tries to watch, gets a more limited view (and, possibly, a crick in the neck).

So why not let science aid nature, and use a mirror? You'll both get a chance to view the "greatest show on earth" for a change, and the man will get a different perspective on the whole affair, too. Here are a few ways you might use a mirror:

- Stand in front of a large mirror, fully clothed, while you embrace and kiss.
- While watching each other in the mirror, slowly undress each other.
- Still standing, each partner can take turns kissing the other, from mouth down the body to the feet and back up again. The passive partner can watch in the mirror while the active one does all the work.
- Stand behind your partner as he or she faces the mirror. Then use your hands to caress whatever body parts take your fancy while your partner watches in the mirror.
- Watch each other perform oral sex. Kneel before your partner as he or she faces the mirror. You not only get the intense pleasure of having your genitals kissed and sucked, but you can watch the entire show at the same time.
- Have sex with the man entering from behind as the woman kneels on the floor in front of the mirror, sideways to the mirror. She can look to one side to see a view closer to that which her partner is always able to see.

How about viewing sex in bed, though? You may need to go out of your way a little, if you don't happen to have a mirror conveniently positioned next to your bed. Of course if you happen to have a four-poster with a mirror ceiling, you are ready for action. (Many waterbed stores sell very nice king-sized waterbeds with mirrored ceilings, so such things are not hard to come by . . . assuming you've got the available cash, of course.) A mirrored ceiling allows more angles of view; you might have sex with the man on his back, the woman on top of him on her back, too, both of you looking up at yourselves on the ceiling, watching the motion of the penis as it works its way in and out. Or take turns watching. The woman on the bottom, man on top facing her, later the woman on top facing the man. Each gets to watch the other's back, which may not sound as erotic as some positions, but the mere novelty of the situation, the unusual, voyeuristic view of your own sex act is likely to be highly erotic.

You might position a large mirror at the foot or side of the bed. Many furniture stores sell tall wheeled mirrors (no doubt for just such a purpose). In fact you could try using two or three of these mirrors, to provide several different views. You'll have a chance of seeing what's going on wherever you happen to be.

You might also install a mirror on your ceiling. However, make sure it's done according to the building codes—the last thing you want is fifty pounds of glass dropping on you while you're making love! If you are not absolutely sure of what you are doing, have someone else do it for you. (This should provide amusement for the local handyman, and a great new story for his buddies.) In fact in some states it's illegal to install a mirror on the ceiling, for this very reason (though how the mirror police are likely to find out we can't imagine). At one time it was possible to buy a lightweight flexible mirror—a shiny

The Best Sex of Your Life

reflective surface, not glass—that could be safely attached to the ceiling, though we haven't seen them for sale for some time.

You could also try using a large hand mirror. You could take turns using the mirror, angling it so you can watch whatever pleases you. For many people it's a very unusual sensation, and very exciting, viewing the sex act at close quarters with a mirror. Watch the penis slide in and out of the vagina slowly, withdraw the penis completely and watch the vaginal lips remain partially open, as if waiting for the penis to re-enter. Put the penis back into the vagina and watch the vaginal lips pull on the penis . . . all this can be highly arousing. So exciting, in fact, that in some cases it can provoke an early orgasm.

Some men have reported that closely viewing their partner's vaginal area had an unexpected result. The women, although perhaps initially uncomfortable, eventually felt more at ease, to such a degree that they were able to orgasm through sex with their partners, something they couldn't do before.

Some couples will never try mirrors. They probably feel that they're in no condition to be watching each other, that it's safer in the dark. Others, however, report that it's an erotic experience even if the reflection in the mirror shows a couple of bodies that are in far from athletic or movie-star condition. Give it a try; you might like it. And if you like mirrors, you'll love video! (See Module 22.)

Sexual Position #19

This may be a pleasing position in front of a mirror, from the woman's point of view. With the mirror at the end of the bed, she can watch his penis as it slips in and out of her, a view she's normally denied. The man gets the view of her buttocks bouncing up and down, a very agreeable sight for most men. He can also use his hands to caress her buttocks, legs, and back. She may wish to lean forward, holding onto his legs to steady herself.

Module 22

Home Video Erotica

*I*f you own a video recorder, you may have already thought about what we're about to talk about—creating your own home videos. No, not just birthdays, vacations, and visits to your family. But bedroom (or living room, or kitchen) activities.

You might think most people would be embarrassed at having sex in front of a camera. In fact, the opposite is true in many cases. One of the men in our survey confessed to taping his own videos, at home with his wife. He was surprised at her reaction to the camera: "She really gets turned on and will try almost anything in front of the camera. She will go down on me in a ferocious animal-like way. She even swallows my come and when we play the recordings back on our TV she gets just as excited as before. Through the miracle of electronic technology we are able to enhance our lovemaking in our own bedroom." There, you knew the electronics revolution had to have a deeper significance than providing you with the ability to tape your in-laws at Thanksgiving.

The reaction of this man's wife is not an unusual one. Many couples have found that recording themselves making love is an extremely erotic experience. Some people are a little concerned about, well, let's say, *security*. They don't like the idea of the existence of a tape showing them in the most intimate of situations. In fact for this reason you may never be able to get your partner to agree. To a great extent it's a matter of trust, though. Assure your partner that there will be only one tape. The first time you might agree that you will tape your lovemaking, view the tape, and then tape *I Love Lucy* over the top. Once your partner is more comfortable with the idea, he or she may be prepared to keep the tape, and for good reason. Viewing the tape later can bring back the excitement all over again.

Today's video cameras are quite capable of recording in dimly lit rooms, so don't think you'll have to perform in the glare of bright lights. You may be surprised at how good you both look in low lights—there's no need to be in perfect condition before you begin.

And just how *do* you begin? You'll need a tripod, of course, so you can position the camera at just the right place and angle. You could view a few professional pornographic movies first, to get a few ideas—though most professional pornographic movies are rather short on ideas, unfortunately, unless you manage to find one of the really good ones. (We'll discuss how to do that in Module 29.) Some couples who really get into moviemaking prepare a small script, adding a variety of fantasies—light bondage, perhaps—and create a collection of tapes. ("What shall we view tonight, dear? *Bondage in Suburbia, or Nurse Nancy at Night?*")

Do whatever comes to mind. The first movie you make will not appear professional by any means. But as you get used to the camera you'll find that you begin to perform for it, and will feel less self-conscious. You'll also get better at anticipating where the camera should point, and at making sure you stay within camera view.

You'll get better at figuring out what works best on the sound track, too. Try a little background music while you tape, and place a microphone near you on the bed, too. The sounds of passion can be very sensual, and will add to your viewing pleasure later.

Half the pleasure of making these movies is a feeling of exhibitionism, getting "down and dirty" on film. Of course the idea is to create something you can view later. You could watch the tape all the way through, playing with each other as you view it. Or you may want to copy the action on the screen, doing on your bed or living room floor what you can see yourselves doing on the TV screen.

Oh, one more thing. Once you've made a tape, be careful where you leave it! Don't let it get mixed up with your favorite soap operas or cable movies, or you may create pleasure for a visitor, and a great deal of embarrassment for yourselves.

Sexual Position #20

Tonight, a position you might use to view your home movies. It's not a good "thrusting" position, but it allows a couple to sit and view the action on TV while the man caresses the woman's breasts and legs and kisses the back of her neck. He'll probably want to be sitting against the headboard or the wall or, if the viewing is in the living room, perhaps sitting on the sofa. She can wiggle around on his lap to get his attention, and squeeze his penis with her vagina. If you really feel the need for a little thrusting, she can push up with her arms and legs, and he can help by lifting her buttocks.

Module 23

Your Lover as Dessert

Sex has always been related in some way to food. Typical courting activity includes the man taking the woman out to eat. Even for couples who have been together for years, going out for a romantic meal is often a prelude to sex. And anyway, sex is a physical lust, an animal lust, similar in many ways to a hunger for food. American author F. Scott Fitzgerald put it like this: "The kiss originated when the first male reptile licked the first female reptile, implying in a subtle, complimentary way that she was as succulent as the small reptile he had for dinner the night before."

So why not combine the two, the kisses and the dinner. There's no need to go out for a romantic meal, though. Why not eat at home? And if food and sex are linked, why not make the link closer than ever.

Place a large terry cloth towel or two on top of your bed, and lay your lover down on top. You might want to also tie your lover down—gently tie his or her hands and ankles to the bed with ribbons or some other soft material. Make sure the room is warm, of course.

Next, bring a warm wet towel and lightly massage your lover's body. Rub his or her body all over—it'll feel good—and pay particular attention to the areas of the body that you plan to use as your "plat du jour." Now smear a little instant chocolate icing (or whatever flavor you prefer), on the nipples. Top it with instant whipped cream and a couple of cherries.

Smear some of your favorite after-dinner liqueur on your partner's belly and thighs, turn on some romantic music, and slowly savor your dessert. Use your tongue and mouth to lick and swirl and mix the tastes of the confection with the tastes of your lover's body.

What else might you use? You are limited by nothing but your imagination. Ice cream tastes good to the eater, and has the added advantage of providing a little chill of excitement to the eatee, too. Honey is tasty; dollop it onto the penis and then suck it off. Whipped topping on the vagina provides a nice excuse to thoroughly lick the vaginal lips, and you may even want to gently insert food into the vagina. A grape inserted into the vagina might be pushed out by the woman's PC muscles (see Module 1) into the man's mouth, for instance. Still, use some common sense here. You'd better agree beforehand what food can be inserted, and foods that are spicy or acidic have no place near the genitals! And don't be greedy—after you've had your dessert, switch roles and let your partner dine.

By the way, before we leave the subject of your partner as food, a quick word about oral sex. Most couples limit themselves to oral sex before intercourse. They consider oral sex afterward—in particular cunnilingus—to be too messy, too smelly. (And in any case, the typical sexual scenario for many couples is "oral sex, intercourse, go to sleep," so by the time you've finished intercourse the sex is probably over!) Oral sex after intercourse is often a very musky experience for the man, and may be a taste that has to be acquired. However, couples who do indulge in post-intercourse cunnilingus often enjoy a new experience, a taste and smell that is highly sexual and arousing. The man may eat his partner, then suck her nipples, lick her neck, and kiss her. The smell of sex is transferred to those parts of her body, and can be extremely arousing. If the couple continues with another bout of intercourse, the smell and taste of their sex provide a further stimulus; they seem to be somehow enveloped in sex.

Sexual Position #21

There are a couple of ways to get into this position. This might be a natural progression from a position with the man on top of the woman, entering her from the rear. He can roll to his side, pulling her over with him, and then roll all the way onto his back, so she's lying on top of him. Or start with him lying on his back; the woman kneels over his penis, facing away from him, and inserts his penis into her. Then she leans back all the way until she's lying on top of him.

He can thrust gently by rocking his hips. The really nice thing about this position is that he can easily caress her breasts and touch her clitoris and vaginal area. The combination of the penis pressing on the front wall of the vagina, onto the G spot, and his hands touching her can be extremely pleasurable.

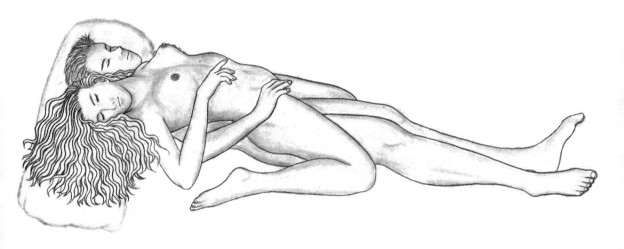

Module 24

Dirty Dancing

We all know dancing can be erotic. It was once described as "a vertical expression of a horizontal desire," and according to the Kinsey data sixty percent of men and fifty percent of women find themselves sexually aroused by close dancing. After all, isn't that why many people go dancing, to find a mate—for a lifetime or a night? Few women haven't experienced an erect penis pressed against them during a slow dance.

But even if you don't find yourself getting sexually aroused during dancing, it provides the romance that women want; you can consider dancing as part of extended foreplay or arousal. Close dancing can be intimate and romantic, and that's always helpful when trying to get a woman interested in sex . . . which is why so many men (and women) take dancing lessons to meet a prospective mate.

So, why not go out for a night's dancing? What sort? Well, any kind you've found to be sexually exciting in the past. Some kinds of dancing are more erotic than others, though. Close dancing is more erotic than disco, though some disco dances allow the partners a certain amount of rubbing of legs and thighs. It can also give you a degree of voyeurism, as you can stand back and view your lover's body . . . though to be fair it's usually more erotic for the man, as most men don't dance well enough to appear particularly sensual. (Why did disco dancing evolve along with the sexual revolution? Perhaps because young people no longer needed an excuse to hold a member of the opposite sex.) Ballroom and country and western dancing can provide opportunities for closeness and holding that can be arousing—many people find the tango, in particular, to be a very romantic, even erotic, dance.

If you've never been to a reggae bar, you might want to try it. (If you *have* been to one, you may already recognize the erotic potential.) Reggae provides an opportunity for dancing closely and rhythmically, with one knee between the partner's legs. Reggae is rooted in a heavy bass rhythm, and dancers often dance very close, using a rocking motion back and forth. A leg between your partner's legs will almost certainly be arousing. Keep this up for two or three hours and he's likely to end up with an erection to rival anything he's had before, and she may be so wet it becomes obvious. Many American cities have reggae bars—take a look in the local entertainment guide.

Another form of dancing that can be very erotic is calypso, though unfortunately this is not widely available in the United States. In Trinidad, for instance, a dance called *whining* is very popular. In this dance the woman faces away from the man. He dances right behind her, with his crotch pressed against her buttocks; she dances with her hands in the air, and her body slightly bent at the middle so that her buttocks are pushed into his crotch, rhythmically grinding against the penis. (Those Caribbean islanders really know how to have fun!) The strange thing is that this dance, which is quite clearly sexual in nature (how can the man possibly avoid getting an erection from this dance?), is regarded as quite acceptable even in a "family" atmosphere. The sight of parents sitting happily while their teenage daughters "whine" with their boyfriends, undoubtedly raising the boys' expectations and organs, is truly strange.

While dancing closely and slowly you can nibble each other's ears, kiss and nibble necks and cheeks. It's fun to be a little risqué while dancing, too. Grab your partner's tush now and again, hold your partner's buttocks tightly and pull his or her crotch into yours. Kiss deeply and passionately during the slow dances. Just how explicit you want to get will depend on how easily embarrassed you are, and how bright the lights are.

You don't have to go out to dance, of course. Dance a little at home. That way you can choose exactly the music you want, and do whatever you want without fear of embarrassing yourselves (assuming you've got your kids out of the way somehow, that is). You might try some reggae and calypso, for instance, in the privacy of your own home, though part of the fun of such music is the atmosphere of the club in which it's played.

Just slow dance to any music you like. Take your time, and get into the rhythm and romanticism of the dancing. Kiss and fondle each other while you dance. You can slowly undress each other, too, and dance naked for a while, but take your time. See how long you can tease each other before you go all the way. If you match each other in size, you can even attempt intercourse while dancing. Imagine whining with your partner while connected—dirty dancing at its best! (Be careful, though; make sure the motions aren't too wild or someone might get hurt or, worse, bent out of shape!)

If the woman is tall, a couple may be able to dance face to face, with his penis inside her vagina. If she's very light and the man quite strong, he could even pick her up—she can wrap her legs around him while he dances.

Sexual Position #22

Speaking of sex while dancing, the next page shows a nice little standing position you can use. This is pretty much what *whining* looks like (only with your clothes off), a nice position to try while dancing to calypso. (Actually it's nice when dancing to pretty much anything, or when not dancing at all!) The woman should take care not to "shake her booty" too vigorously, or you'll both get hurt. But a little shaking around will be very exciting for both of you, and you'll soon get into a rhythm that you both find sensuous. It's a great view for the man, too. (All the penetration-from-behind positions are exciting for a man though. The view of his penis as it grinds in and out of his lover is something that few men can resist, and something that few women understand—unless they try working with a mirror . . . see Module 21.)

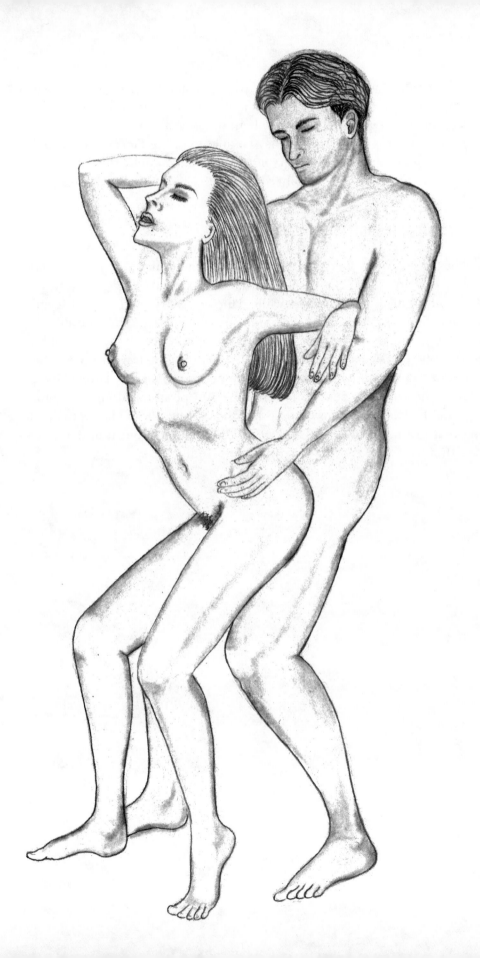

Module 25

Bath Night!

*I*t's a bath night. Time to get all soaped up together. Bathing together is another activity that many couples enjoy early in their relationship, but seem to forget about later. It's a wonderful experience, though, well worth revisiting.

Or course it doesn't have to be an actual bath; a shower can be very pleasant too. The bath has the advantage that you can take your time, lie back and enjoy the warmth and some gentle kissing and touching before you do anything too active. You could also take a bottle of wine and some cheese and crackers with you, and really make a meal of it. Of course you need a decent size tub, something large enough for both of you to lie in without feeling like a couple of sardines.

If you are going to bathe or shower together, don't wash yourselves . . . that defeats the object of the exercise. Rather, wash each other. Begin with the non-genital areas—soap each other's backs and arms. Don't treat this as a purely utilitarian wash, though. Soap up your partner's body and use the lovely slipperiness to massage and caress. Spend a little extra time on your partner's breasts or chest . . . don't forget that you can be kissing while you are doing this. You'll eventually make your way to the genitals . . . and don't forget the anus, of course. It's a wonderful feeling to have your partner soaping up your genitals and gently washing and rinsing.

It's probably a good idea to wash each other in turn. With both of you at work at the same time you'll find arms getting entwined and in the way. Allow one partner to simply enjoy the attention, while the other does the work, then swap.

If possible, try intercourse. All that rubbing should have aroused both of you. One problem, though, is that most baths are too small to be comfortable for sex. If yours is big enough, you might manage it. In fact, the water may provide enough flotation to allow some unusual positions. If you are in the shower, it's usually fairly easy to have intercourse. The woman can lean against the wall and hold onto the soap dish or shower head (though don't put too much pressure onto these things, as they may come away from the wall during the heat of your passion). The man can then enter her from behind—he may need to open his legs wide and bend his knees, to bring himself down to the correct height. When you've finished, you can wash each other again, then dry off and retire to bed.

❧ ❧ Sex in Water ❧ ❧

Sex in water can be very pleasant, as you eliminate, to some degree, the effects of gravity. You can perform the standing intercourse positions with ease, whereas in normal gravity you'd quickly tire. (It's been suggested that one day zero-gravity sex will be all the rage, but until that day the closest you'll get to it is making love in water.) The problem is, *where?* As we mentioned earlier, sex in a bath is often difficult, because most people have rather small baths. You'll find yourself limited to a rather small range of sexual positions, or you may decide it's simply not worth the trouble. If you are lucky enough to have a very large tub, great, but what you really need is a hottub or a spa.

Some couples enjoy sex in the sea, sometimes at night, though you can also do it during the day if you are very discreet. Enter the water in your bathing suits, walk out until you are quite deep, then pull the bottom halves aside to reveal penis and vagina. You can have sex yet appear to be involved in nothing more than a passionate embrace.

Sexual Position #23

This is exactly the type of position that is easier under water than above. It's also the type of position that can be used at a beach. With almost all of your body under water nobody can see what you are really up to; you may be kissing, but what's going on below the surface? Who knows?

If you try this out of water, though, be careful; you wouldn't want to drop her and pull something off! In fact, you won't want to try this out of water unless he's reasonably strong and she's not too heavy. That's the nice thing

about water; it will let people try positions that they are physically incapable of carrying out on dry land.

To use this position, she starts by lifting a leg while he bends his knees to lower himself. He enters her, and she brings her legs up to his waist. When he grabs and lifts her buttocks, she wraps her legs around his waist and her arms around his neck. He now uses his hands to rock her on his penis; she can assist with her arms and legs. Have fun, but be careful.

Module 26

Undressing Each Other

oes the following sound like the beginning of a normal sexual routine for you? You undress, your partner undresses, you both get into bed, and you have sex. What ever happened to undressing each other? Remember the passion for each other that was so strong there was no way you could keep your hands off your partner long enough to take your clothes off? No, you were interested in getting your hands on your partner's body, you didn't care about yours. Luckily your partner was just as interested in putting his or her hands on your body, so it worked out fine; you undressed your partner, and your partner undressed you.

Undressing each other is like so many sexual "techniques" that we didn't even know were techniques. We did it naturally, in the heat of passion . . . and when the passion started to fade, we stopped doing it, without even noticing. The undressing ritual can be the perfect start of arousal. Like everything else with sex, though, don't rush it. You don't simply want to swap roles, and end up stripping each other as quickly as you strip yourselves. No, the point is to do this slowly, lingeringly. Begin by embracing and kissing. Rub each other through your clothes. Caress each other's buttocks. He can reach for her breasts, she can squeeze his bulge. Then slowly begin undoing bits and pieces; help your partner pull off a sweater, for instance. Gradually unbutton shirts and blouses; then, while you continue kissing, let your hands slip inside and caress your partner's body.

The man can undo her bra and lean forward to take a nipple in his mouth; she can unzip him and slip her hand around his penis, or squeeze his testicles. With your partner's pants loosened, slide a hand in and feel the buttocks. Let your hand slip between the crack and take a handful of cheek . . . and squeeze. Take off pants before you remove shirts; there's something quite erotic about being partly dressed with the most erogenous zones exposed. With his underpants still on, she can kneel down, pull his penis out, and take him in her mouth for a few moments—just gently suck for a little while. He can kneel down and lick the crease where her legs join her body, gently nibble her inner thighs, rub his face over her vagina, still covered by the panties. Perhaps he might pull the material aside and enjoy a quick lick of her vaginal lips.

When you remove your partner's shirt or blouse, wait for a while before you pull anything else off. Spend a little time touching and kissing the exposed skin, caressing your partner's back, kissing his or her shoulders. The idea of undressing each other is to *slowly* reveal more of your partner's body, and to show appreciation and enjoyment as you do so.

⚜ ⚜ Don't Take It All Off! ⚜ ⚜

If you really enjoy this game you can develop it somewhat. Don't simply remove all your clothes and then jump into bed. You may want to leave pieces of clothing on throughout your lovemaking. In fact you may even want to get *changed* into underclothing you know will work well for your sex games before you get undressed. For instance, the woman might dress in regular outer garb, but beneath wear a G string or crotchless panties, with garter belts and stockings. Or perhaps a bodice that pushes up her breasts but leaves her nipples exposed. The effect on the man is likely to be tremendous, as he slowly removes her normal day clothes to reveal these incredibly sexy undergarments. (If you are going to do this, though, make sure you change clothes where your lover can't see you, or it tends to spoil the effect.)

When you've removed enough clothes to have sex, why bother removing more? If the woman is wearing crotchless panties, you can have sex through them. If she's wearing a G string or even normal everyday panties, the man can pull them aside and enter her; the presence of the clothing during intercourse adds to the atmosphere of sexual abandon. You don't have to remove the man's underwear, either, if you don't want to. You can tug that to one side, too. As for his shirts and her bra, they don't all have to come off. Having sex half-clothed makes a nice change, with different textures against your bodies and a feeling of passion that comes from being more concerned with sex than with removing all obstacles first. Nudity in a long-term relationship can become so routine that it no longer excites, as least not to the degree that it used to. Wearing clothing that exposes a few parts of the body, and leaves other parts to the imagination, can help rekindle the excitement.

❧ ❧ Undressing for Your Partner ❧ ❧

The woman may want to undress *for* her partner, too, to put on a show. She might need a little practice to get it right, and may want to add music, but few men will remain unmoved at the sight of their lover slowly exposing her body to him, doing a striptease. (Of course it helps if you've been following your diet and exercise program to get into shape first!) Apart from the normal visual turn-on of seeing a woman's body, men enjoy the idea that this is *for them,* that the woman is serving him as a concubine in a harem serves her master, or entertaining him as a courtesan might entertain her client. Before the woman begins, she may wish to undress her lover first, get him a little aroused, and then let him lie back and enjoy the show.

Of course the man can do this, too. Unfortunately, though, most men are pretty clumsy at this sort of thing, and would probably be embarrassed to even try. Still, if the man is good at dancing, and willing to try anything, his mate may want to spend a little time training him.

Undressing each other can be very erotic—it's like unwrapping a very special present. So tonight, don't strip like your clothes are on fire. Strip each other slowly, as if you were unwrapping a special present and don't want to spoil the delicious anticipation.

Sexual Position #24

Here's a side-by-side position that has the benefit of allowing you to caress and kiss much of your partner's body during intercourse. She's lying on her back with her knees up. He's on his side next to her with his legs under her knees, and his groin pressed against her buttocks. He can hold onto her hip with one hand, to help steady her while he thrusts into her. Or he can use that hand to caress her body. Many men—and women—enjoy this position because it allows the man to kiss her breasts and suck her nipples during intercourse.

It's also a very tender, intimate position, ideal for gentle kisses on the mouth and quiet, loving conversation. It's a "slow" position, that can help the man delay his orgasm, too. The woman can hold her legs tightly together, to hold him inside her. And by moving her knees up and down, or her legs from side to side, she can adjust the angle of the penis inside her—she may be able to direct it to the G spot.

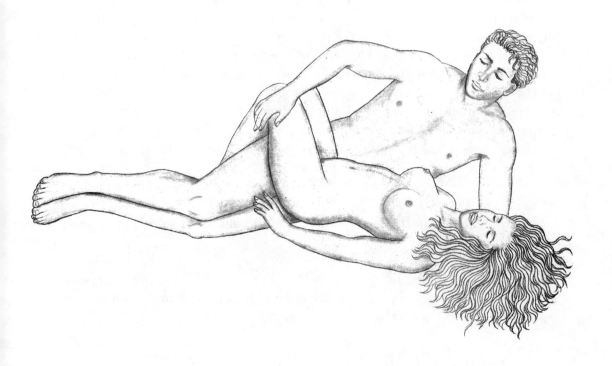

Hugging and Kissing

For this module, try to remember what it was like when you were kids, back in the days when the closest you got to sex was a quick grope, and your main amorous activity was kissing and hugging. It's common for people in long-term relationships to forget about the gentle touching and kissing, and focus their sexual activity almost entirely on more "base" sexual activities—intercourse and oral sex. Maybe it's because during adolescence petting is seen as a substitute for sex—you'd rather be getting laid, but in the meantime petting will do. When you finally reach the point at which sex is more easily available, or even regularly available, you forget about petting and get on with more "adult" sexual activities. This sort of slow arousal is lost in almost all long-term relationships—so all of us can understand Raymond Chandler when he uses the loss as an analogy for drinking. "Alcohol is like love," he said. "The first kiss is magic, the second is intimate, the third is routine. After that you just take the girl's clothes off."

Of course there's nothing wrong with intercourse and oral sex, but if that's the only thing you do you'll miss some great opportunities for slow and erotic sexual arousal . . . and you'll miss an activity that can be very satisfying and sexy in itself. Kissing and touching can be both loving and highly erotic. Some women can "feel" a kiss in their breasts and genitals, and can even have an orgasm from passionate kissing alone. If men realized just how arousing a kiss can be, they'd be much more eager to kiss their partners! "The sound of a kiss is not so loud as that of a cannon," said Justice Oliver Wendell Holmes, "but its echo lasts a great deal longer." (This doesn't seem like Oliver Wendell Holmes' customary subject, but hey, even Supreme Court Justices like to get laid now and then.)

Paradoxically women often don't realize just how important such activities are until they're gone. Early in sexual relationships women are often just as eager to go directly to sexual activities as their mates. Yet later in the relationship they find they miss the hugging, kissing, and tender touching that characterized their courting. Women often respond to sex surveys that lovemaking is far more than just sex and an orgasm; it's also warmth and intimacy and unhurried touching, hugging, and kissing—not just in bed, but in other places and times, too. *Unhurried* is a very important word here. What we are talking about is not kissing and touching immediately prior to sexual intercourse, not the sort of contact that many men regard as necessary in order to get their partners "ready." Rather, we are talking about kissing, hugging, and touching *for the sake* of kissing, hugging, and touching. While these activities may lead to sexual intercourse, try to take pleasure directly from them, and not purely in anticipation of what is about to come.

✄ ✄ Getting Started ✄ ✄

Start the arousal a few hours before bed. When you first meet after the work day, spend several minutes simply hugging and kissing. Why not go out for the evening, with the intention of finding a place for some "heavy petting." Go to a drive-in movie, or go for a romantic meal and then to a lover's lane or another such spot where young lovers go. Maybe you could take a picnic basket and a blanket for a drive into the woods or the beach. Find a quiet and romantic spot where you can be alone.

Begin by hugging and talking with each other. Tell your partner of your love, and follow up with a gentle kiss. Let your kisses and caresses get more passionate. Kiss deeply, touching tongues and caressing the inside of your partner's mouth. Suck and nibble your partner's lips. Don't rush to touch each other's genitals, though. Rather, imagine you are a couple of reticent kids, hormones pushing you toward sex but social constraints holding you back. You might even play a little game; the woman can play the shy virgin, pushing his hands away from her breasts the first few times he tries to caress them, keeping her legs closed until the passion carries her away.

Take your time. Kiss each other's neck and face, and nibble the ears. Take your lover's face in your hands, hold your partner close while you kiss deeply. Remember how you kissed when you were first in love, and kiss with that degree of passion. You'll find the memories coming back and the passion rising.

Vary the "tempo" of the kisses—one moment gentle and very light, the next moment more firm and passionate.

Eventually you'll want to go further, of course. Touch each other through your clothes (remember the first time you squeezed a girl's breast through her blouse, or felt a boy's bulge in his jeans?). Don't go directly to the genitals, though. The man can squeeze his partner's breasts, she can feel his chest and squeeze his inner thighs while the back of her hand brushes against his penis and testicles.

Keep going as long as you can stand it, until you're just bursting with sexual tension. Eventually you'll have to release some clothing. Unbutton her blouse and suck her nipples, unbutton his pants and fondle his penis. Whatever you do, don't get carried away and go all the way to intercourse. He should use his hand to touch her vagina and clitoris, to slip a finger inside her. Try to remember what it was like the very first time you touched a woman there. She should masturbate him, pumping his penis with her hand, and occasionally gently squeezing his testicles. Don't perform oral sex—though the woman might use her mouth to quickly lubricate her partner's penis.

At some point one of you will have to lie back and take it, as your partner brings you to orgasm. When you've got over your orgasm, return the favor and help your partner to orgasm, too. When it's all over, though, don't rush home. Stay a while, kissing and cuddling and telling each other how much you love one another, and how much you enjoyed your petting session. *Then* rush home and have intercourse!

Sexual Position #25

This position is a sort of reversal of the Sexual Position #17 in Module 19. The woman's on top, but his legs are apart and hers are closed. If she holds them tight and contracts her PC muscles she can create a nice tight fit. He can open his legs quite wide and hold her buttocks to pull her down onto his penis. The pelvic regions will be rubbing tightly together, too, providing good stimulation for the clitoris and vaginal area. Of course the other advantage of this position is that it's a great hugging and kissing position.

The Search for the G Spot

*I*t's time for a little exploration, a search for a sexual treasure. In this module we're going to talk about the G spot. We'll discuss what it is, what it can do for you, and how to find it.

It's often said that the first person to describe the G spot was a German obstetrician and gynecologist named Dr. Ernst Gräfenberg. Indeed the full name of the G spot is the *Gräfenberg spot,* named for this "discoverer" who first noticed it in 1944 while researching contraceptives. However, something like this can't go totally unnoticed for millennia, and in fact there are references to such a thing at other times and places—Gräfenberg really didn't discover it, you might say he rediscovered it. Actually, Regnier de Graaf, a Dutch anatomist, described the G spot way back in the seventeenth century. Still, the G spot was until recently unknown to most doctors (even to most owners!), and even now there are many people who are skeptical about its existence.

What exactly is the G spot? It's an area of very sensitive tissue inside the vagina—about halfway up on the anterior (front) wall. This area swells when aroused; some women describe the G spot as even more sensitive than the clitoris. It seems to be a bundle of blood vessels, glands, ducts, and nerve endings that enlarge when stimulated. The soft tissue hardens and becomes quite well defined, and can do so very quickly.

In fact this explains why many doctors don't believe the G spot exists; unless the G spot has been stimulated, it's not visible, so doctors who have spent their professional lives studying a woman's reproductive organs—carrying out gynecological examinations and surgery, for instance—are often skeptical. They've never seen anything there, so it can't be there.

Stimulation of the G spot causes a very different sexual sensation for the woman, and can also lead to ejaculation of a semen-like fluid from the urethra. Until recently female ejaculation was thought by many doctors to be a foolish myth, but there's now no doubt that it exists. While women may ejaculate from clitoral stimulation, or vaginal sex without specific stimulation of the G spot, it's more likely to happen if the G spot is being directly stimulated. The amount of fluid expelled varies greatly, from a few drops—almost unnoticeable—to a teaspoon or two. Some women claim to ejaculate a cup or two of fluid, though these accounts are almost certainly exaggerations.

Female ejaculation has caused great embarrassment for many women and their partners. It's often ascribed to urination. In fact, it's similar in composition to a man's ejaculate, to the fluid expelled by the prostate. The ejaculate seems to contain glucose and a prostatic acid, along with urea and creatine. Think of it like this: It's a perfectly natural occurrence for a woman to ejaculate, but because few people know how to stimulate the G spot, it's something that most women don't experience. Those who understand it and have experienced it, often find it very erotic. After all, it's associated with intense excitement on the part of the woman—it's quite natural for a man to feel excited, too, by being able to bring his partner to such a level of ecstasy that she ejaculates.

While a woman may be able to reach her G spot while sitting or kneeling, it's often quite difficult for her to do so while lying down, at least without some kind of sexual toy. The G spot is located well inside her vagina, on the front wall. Her partner can reach it with a finger or penis (no, not with his tongue!), or she can reach it with a dildo, but it may be difficult to reach it with her own fingers.

❦ ❦ *Let's Play Doctor* ❦ ❦

Okay, let's see if we can find the G spot. Begin with kissing and cuddling, and a little gentle petting. When the woman is ready, she lies on her back with her legs spread, while her partner kneels before her, or to one side of her. With the palm of his hand facing up, he gently inserts one or two fingers (his index or middle finger) about two inches into her vagina, and carefully rubs the front wall of the vagina (the wall that is "up," as she's lying on her back). The man should explore this region of the vagina with the flat of his finger, being careful not to scrape with his fingernail, of course. He's feeling for an area about half way between the pubic bone and the end of the vagina—at first there may be nothing there, but as the G spot becomes aroused it will swell and harden. The man can gently press downward with his other hand on the woman's abdomen, at the pubic hairline, to further stimulate the G spot. As he presses with both sets of fingers—down with the fingers on her abdomen, up with the fingers inside her vagina—he may feel a small lump between the fingers. It may start with the size of a small bean, then grow to the size of a quarter or even larger.

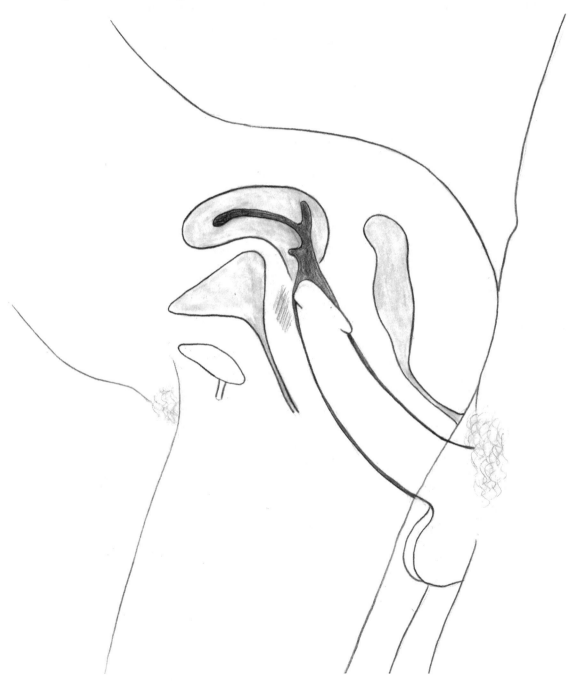

Of course the woman should provide feedback, to let her partner know when he's hit the spot. The G spot will need more firm stimulation than is used for the clitoris; while the clitoris generally requires very gentle touching, the G spot not only tolerates but actually *needs* a firmer touch. She may feel a very unusual internal sensation during the stimulation of the G spot, a feeling that is quite different from the sexual feelings to which she is accustomed. Many women feel a little uncomfortable the first time the G spot is stimulated, as if they want to urinate. She may also feel contractions in her uterus.

If you continue stimulating the G spot in this manner until orgasm, the woman may ejaculate her seminal-like fluid. You'll notice that it has no odor and is a cloudy white fluid—nothing like urine!

By the way, some men find it very exciting to perform cunnilingus while stimulating the G spot. Kneeling before her the man can rub with a couple of fingers inside her, while at the same time leaning forward and licking her clitoris and vaginal lips.

Here's another position you may try to stimulate the G spot; the woman can lie on her belly, with her legs apart and her pelvis angled so her vagina is turned upward a little. Now the man inserts a finger or two—the palm downward—and rubs the front wall of the vagina. An advantage of this position is that after playing with the G spot in this manner for a while, the man can then insert his penis. As we'll see in a moment, this is a good position for intercourse, as the penis can stimulate the G spot from this angle. The only drawback to this position is that it may be awkward for the man to stimulate the G spot with his fingers, as he may find the angle at which he has to hold his hand to be uncomfortable.

✳ ✳ Intercourse Positions for G-Spot Stimulation ✳ ✳

Not all intercourse positions stimulate the G spot well. Some rear-entry positions do, as does the *oceanic* position. And a woman-on-top position can provide the control that the woman needs to direct the man's penis to the G spot.

The rear-entry position, with the woman on all fours and the man entering her from behind, may work well. The head of the penis will be directed toward the front wall of the vagina—the woman can move her hips into a position that best presents the G spot to the head of the penis. The man may be able to reach around with his hand and further stimulate the clitoris and vaginal lips.

The *oceanic* position, which we looked at back in Module 9, can also direct the penis to the G spot, and the man is also able to press gently on his partner's belly during intercourse.

A woman-on-top position, though, allows the woman more control. Because she's able to lean in whatever direction she wishes, she can "use" the man's penis for her own pleasure, controlling exactly where the head of the penis rubs, how deep it strokes, and how quickly.

If you use a diaphragm for birth control, you should know that it may block stimulation of the G spot. For some women it does, for some it doesn't. If you find that it *does*, you have a couple of options; find another form of birth control, or have the man stimulate the G spot with his fingers before you insert the diaphragm.

By the way, some women report that once they know where the G spot is, they can masturbate by rubbing the G spot through their body—that is, by rubbing on the abdomen, as we described earlier in our little G-spot exploration. Some women masturbate using one hand to stimulate the clitoris, and the other to stimulate the G spot through the abdomen.

Sexual Position #26

What more apt position for this module than one that stimulates the G spot? A rear-entry position such as this directs the penis toward the G spot. Because the vagina is angled up a little—more so than it would be if the woman were kneeling down with her elbows on the same surface (kneeling on the bed itself, for instance), the penis is more likely to rub the G spot. The woman can change the angle further, by pushing up on her hands, or by lying closer to the bed, to get the position just right.

A Night at the Movies

*T*onight's the night for a trip to the movies. Don't go out, though. Stay in, load an erotic movie into your VCR, and get together on the sofa. Men may be reluctant to raise the issue of watching an erotic or pornographic movie with their partners, but they might be surprised to learn that many, perhaps most, women enjoy them (at least, they enjoy watching a well-made, sensual movie; I'll talk about that in more detail in a few moments). Some surveys have found that as many as eighty-five percent of American women have viewed an "adult" or "pornographic" movie, and that almost half continue to watch them now and again.

Probably many of those women are watching movies just to please their male partners. But it's also true that many women really do get turned on by watching. Watching other people have sex is erotic for most people, even if many of us don't care to admit it. While women in particular generally don't like to admit to being turned on by the sight of two or more people sexually entwined, they are almost as likely to be aroused by it as men. As *The Joy of Sex* states, "most normal people enjoy looking at sex books and reading sex fantasies, which is why abnormal people have to spend so much time and money suppressing them." Of course the same goes for sex movies; they're sexually exciting to most people.

You can find adult movies in many places. Many neighborhood video stores and rental places have adult sections. You'll find them in stores that sell sex toys, too. You can also call Movies Unlimited (800-466-8437), Excalibur (800-289-6684), Video Age (800-279-1555), and Leisure Time Products (800-874-8960) or buy them through the companies we mentioned in Module 17 and through ads in many men's magazines.

✢ ✢ Watch Out for the Bad Ones! ✢ ✢

Unfortunately, there's a significant problem with pornographic movies—most of them are absolutely awful. They're often badly filmed, poorly lit, and about as sensual as wrestling with a skunk. The acting is atrocious, and the plot might best be described as "Hi! Let's Fuck!" Most porn movies are made in a few hours, literally. While Marilyn Chambers, perhaps the most famous adult-movie star, only made five films, the actors these days make literally hundreds of movies during their relatively short careers—two or three hundred movies are not unusual. Each movie is thrown together in a single day. Whatever the "characters" are doing in the movie, it's often the movie itself that really sucks.

Men don't have too many problems with such movies; men are so easy to turn on anyway, the fact that the movie has a plot that could have been written by the apes in *Congo* doesn't seem to matter too much. But it's different for women. While many women can be turned on by pornographic movies, they often find the average movie rather repulsive; too stupid, too ugly, too downright *un*erotic.

But there *are* good movies, erotic movies that women can enjoy. It's just a matter of finding them. One way to find good movies is through The Sexuality Library. This is a company run by women (the same people who run Good Vibrations, a sex-toy store). All the movies they sell are viewed by the women owners and employees, and a review of each one is published in their catalog. Even the women answering the sales phone have reviewed many of the movies, so they can help you find one that you'll like. You can get a catalog by calling The Sexuality Library at 800-289-8423 or 415-974-8990. (Ask for the Good Vibrations catalog at the same time.)

You should also call 800-456-5683 to get the Femme catalog. This company sells videos produced for women and designed to be sensual. It's run by Candida Royalle, who used to act in the normal run-of-the-mill porn movie directed by men, but who decided she wanted to create movies that were truly erotic.

You can also find movie reviews to help you pick the good ones; many men's magazines review movies. They generally do so with a male point of view, of course, though they don't usually concentrate purely on the action. The reviews often say that a particular movie has a stupid plot, unbelievable dialogue, and so on. You'll also sometimes find reviews and ads from companies selling the more sensuous movies in erotic publications such as Libido (800-495-1988, or http://www.indra.com/libido on the World Wide Web) and Paramour (617-499-0069 or http://www2.xensei.com/paramour on the Web).

✿ ✿ Settle Down . . . ✿ ✿

Once you've found what promises to be a good erotic movie, spend a few minutes in preparation. Move the TV and VCR into the bedroom, or perhaps set

up the living room to be more comfortable for sex; place some blankets and pillows around so you can cuddle up together comfortably.

A comfortable position to begin may be with the man sitting on the floor, leaning against a sofa, while the woman sits between his legs, leaning back on him. Both are facing the TV so they can get a good view; and he can caress her breasts and abdomen while they watch, and nibble her ears and neck.

You probably won't want popcorn with this movie, though perhaps a bottle of wine might be nice. Then settle down to watch. If you've found a really good movie, it will move slowly toward sex. Movies made by men often reflect the male attitude of sex; the movies jump into sex almost right away. Movies made by women—or at least recommended by women—are likely to reflect a woman's attitude of sex . . . a slower build-up to the sex act.

Watch the movie and do what feels right. Use the movie as a form of arousal; just because the people on screen are having orgasms doesn't mean you have to. Rather, use the visual excitement you get from the movie to slowly build . . . then really go to it when the movie ends.

Sexual Position #27

Here's a position you can use while watching a movie, using a large ottoman or a daybed. She lies on her front, facing the TV, legs either side of the ottoman. He enters her from behind; again, legs either side of the ottoman. A nice position to stimulate the G spot, and he can move slowly, grasping her hips, as you both watch the action on-screen.

Module 30

Prostate Play

In Module 28 we took a close look at the G spot. The G spot is sometimes described as the female prostate. Not surprisingly, the male prostate is also extremely sensitive, and intimately involved in orgasm and ejaculation, though most men are unaware of its presence or even the correct pronunciation of its name (it's the prost*ate*, not the prost*rate*).

The prostate produces some of the fluid in semen and pushes it into the urethra (the tube that carries the semen to the end of the penis) immediately before ejaculation. The prostate contracts rhythmically, providing that "Oh God, *here it comes!*" feeling just as the orgasm begins.

So the prostate is essential to the sexual process. However, it's not normally directly stimulated in the same way that the G spot is. The G spot may be stimulated by the penis (in some positions), by the fingers, and even by massaging the abdomen. The prostate is, well . . . a little harder to get to.

Actually many people don't much like the idea of directly stimulating the prostate, because in order to do so a finger or some other object must be inserted into the anus. However, that's not to say that prostate stimulation is rare. According to Shere Hite, writing in *Male Sexuality*, thirty-one percent of heterosexual men have tried prostate stimulation, and most of them enjoyed it. Simple anal stimulation is probably even more common. Many couples insert a finger into the anus during sex, even if they are not trying to directly stimulate the prostate. (Both men and women can enjoy anal stimulation.)

But why bother stimulating the prostate? After all, it does its job quite well without any help, doesn't it? Well, yes, but by accident of nature it's a fact that direct stimulation of the prostate can lead to longer and more intense orgasms. And it's in the nature of man to seek intense sexual pleasure in general, and longer and more intense orgasms in particular. For instance, one man in our study said this: "Once during finger penetration she massaged my prostate and I actually orgasmed without having an erection. On another occasion she sucked my penis and massaged my prostate—I had the most glorious orgasm ever." Another man described the feeling of an orgasm during intercourse or oral sex while his partner was touching his prostate as "fantastic."

If you want to find out what all the fuss is about, and have decided to try prostate stimulation (and have a willing partner, of course), here's how. The following procedure explains how your partner can stimulate your prostate. If the process feels painful or uncomfortable at any time, discontinue.

1. First, trim the nails of her index and middle fingers, and smooth any rough edges off them.
2. Take a shower together. Thoroughly wash your partner's genitals, rectal area, and up into the anus. Don't make this seem clinical; you can be kissing and caressing while you play.
3. When you've dried off place a sheet or towel over the bed.
4. Start by kissing and caressing in a normal, unhurried way. He may or may not have an erection before you begin to stimulate the prostate.
5. Before you start, position him on his back with his knees up while you liberally coat his rectal area with KY jelly or some other kind of sexual lubricant or sensual oil. (You may want to put on a rubber glove or finger cot—a sort of "finger condom"—to protect both of you.)
6. As you continue to lightly stroke the erection, press gently on his perineum, the area at the base of the penis, between the testicles and anus.
7. Take a little dab of oil, and gently massage it into the anal area. Slowly press your finger into the anus; the man should try to relax and allow the finger to penetrate gradually.
8. The man may notice immediate pleasure; he should continue to relax the anal muscles, but should tell you if you are going too fast. If necessary slow down, or re-lubricate the area.
9. Continue to gently slide your finger in, deeper and deeper, until it is fully inserted. Slowly rotate your finger clockwise, then counterclockwise.
10. You'll be able to feel the side walls of the rectum; you'll notice that it feels very similar to the walls of a vagina.
11. With the flat of your finger, press up and toward your partner's belly button. As you press up against the wall of his rectum, you should feel a small bulge; it's about the size of a walnut, and is located about two inches inside the anal opening (rather like the G spot, right?).

12. His prostate will be very sensitive to the touch, so be gentle. Massage this bulge, and the sensation of his erection will become more intense.

13. Try moving the finger in a circular motion around the prostate, or press gently on the prostate. Ask him what feels good. At the same time you are touching the prostate, remember that dual stimulation can produce an extremely sensual feeling, so caress the head of the penis, too.

14. Try sucking on the head of the penis while you caress the prostate. Prostate stimulation combined with oral sex can produce extremely strong orgasms. Also, prostate stimulation will increase the volume of the ejaculate—this serves to increase the intensity of the orgasm. If you don't like him coming in your mouth, consider bringing him to the brink with your mouth and finishing off the last few moments with your hand.

15. After the orgasm, he'll probably want you to stop prostate stimulation—it may be too intense. Slowly remove your finger. If you were using a glove or cot, you can dispose of it now. Then wash your hands well with warm soapy water.

❧ ❧ External Stimulation of the Prostate ❧ ❧

There's another, more "elegant" way to stimulate the prostate, though it won't produce such intense sensations; it's possible to do it from outside the body. You press firmly on the perineum, the area immediately behind the testicles, with one or more fingers. As you press at this point, the penis will throb and raise up a little. Press rhythmically. Play with it a little to find out the best position, firmness, and frequency of your pressing.

❧ ❧ Rectal Stimulation and Orgasm ❧ ❧

Prostate stimulation is not the only form of rectal stimulation that you might try. Some studies show that as many as forty-seven percent of heterosexual men have been anally penetrated during masturbation or various sexual activities with a partner. Men who have experienced rectal caresses or the insertion of a finger describe the sensation as pleasurable and the orgasm as feeling different but very strong and enjoyable. Men who have *not* experienced such activity are usually quite skeptical and apprehensive about possible odors and mess, and about what their partner would think about them if they suggested such activity.

But this is not simply an activity that men may enjoy; many women enjoy the sensation of rectal stimulation during sex, too. The anus is a highly sensitive area of the body, the most sensitive of erogenous zones for some people. Simple anal stimulation even has a name: *postillionage.* If you decide to try it, you can take comfort in the fact that you are by no means the first person to find sexual pleasure in that area.

The simplest form of anal stimulation is to caress on and around the anus during sex play or intercourse. The woman's natural lubricants can be used to moisten the anus. However, remember that once a finger has touched the anus, it shouldn't go near the vagina. A lubricated finger may also be inserted gently into the anus, and moved gently in and out. Many women enjoy the feeling during intercourse, and men sometimes enjoy the sensation during oral sex.

If you do want to try rectal stimulation, you might find that using a rubber glove or finger cot can reduce any nervousness about the "messiness." (Such nervousness is unnecessary though. Most people find that it's *not* as messy as they first imagined.)

Sexual Position #28

In theory it's possible for the woman to stimulate the prostate during sexual intercourse. Perhaps the best way to try this is using the position shown here. This is a "way station" on the way to the position we saw in Module 13, one of the massage modules. The man begins by lying on top of his partner in the normal "missionary" position. He then swings his legs to one side, and his head and torso to the other, rotating his body until it's at a right angle to his partner.

This may look a little strange, but it's remarkably easy to get into this position. The man may be able to rotate a little further, too, so his buttocks are facing more toward his partner. If she has a tube or tub of lubricant close at hand, she can stimulate his prostate while he thrusts gently in and out. A gentle pelvic rocking motion may be more than enough.

Module 31

Nibbles

Nibbles are nice. The use of the mouth and teeth to nibble and gently bite is very common sex play, not only for humans but for animals, too. Many species use biting as a significant part of their sexual activities. Some researchers have hypothesized that pressure against the lips and teeth may activate a direct nerve connection with the arousal centers, and that the skin may have neural receptors that likewise lead to the arousal centers in the brain and spinal cord. Who knows. We do know, however, that a little nibbling and biting can be quite pleasurable.

The Kinsey data (from The Institute for Sex Research), shows that fifty-five percent of females and fifty percent of males respond erotically when lightly bitten—that is, they get turned on. (They also found that aggressive biting that leaves bite prints on the skin is not effective for most people. Nor is snarling, apparently!) Light biting, sucking, and licking are most erotically stimulating when applied to the throat, sides and back of the neck, ears, upper shoulders and back of shoulders, around the under arms, the breasts (especially the nipples), the abdominal area, the inner thighs, the groin, above and behind the knees, and an inch or two above the knee cap. Gently biting and sucking the fingers and toes are often arousing, too. Alex Comfort, writing in *Joy of Sex,* pointed out that people tend to do what they really want done to them. "Women tend to bite more often than men," he states, "because they enjoy being bitten more than men do." (The Kinsey data agree with this assertion, though the difference is slight, fifty-five percent for women and fifty percent for men.)

The Kama Sutra of Vatsyayana claims that you can bite anywhere that you can kiss—except the upper lip, the interior of the mouth, and the eyes. It seems that there aren't that many places on the body that *don't* feel good when bitten. So here's a rule of thumb; if in doubt, bite! (Gently.) *The Kama Sutra* has half a chapter on biting. (The other half of the chapter explains how to make love to "women of different countries." Did you know, for instance, that "the women of Avantika are fond of foul pleasures, and have not good manners," or that "the women of Aparatika are full of passion, and make slowly the sound *Sit*"? *The Kama Sutra* is probably the most famous of all sex books, yet the least read, because it's just so *strange*.) It describes eight kinds of biting: the hidden bite, the swollen bite, the point, the line of points, the coral and the jewel, the line of jewels, the broken cloud, and the biting of the boar.

❧ ❧ Should You Bite? ❧ ❧

You might want to experiment with a little biting and nibbling. Remember that while most people may enjoy biting, a significant portion don't. So don't be surprised if your partner isn't very happy when you clamp your teeth down on a critical area. Talk about it first. Experiment with very light nibbles and, if your partner enjoys those, take firmer hold. Combine biting with oral sex, too—no firm bites directly on the genitals, of course, but on the inner thighs and abdomen. If your partner enjoys being bitten, you may wish to begin nibbling around the genital area and move gradually into oral sex. You can try very light nibbles on your partner's genitals, too, though be careful with your teeth. It's better in most cases to simply nibble carefully with your lips, and flick with your tongue as you do so, as most people find nips from the teeth to be very uncomfortable, if not downright painful.

What sort of nibbles should you try? Here are a few ideas, but use your imagination (and remember, don't overdo it; your partner will probably prefer a light touch to a very rough one):

- Place the mouth on the flesh, and suck the flesh into your mouth while you press with your teeth.
- With the teeth behind the lips, nibble the flesh.
- Suck firmly on the flesh, pulling it into your mouth, while biting with your teeth. If you suck really hard you will raise the blood to the surface, creating a "hickey" or "love bite." Many lovers enjoy marking their partners, as a sort of mark of possession . . . and find that seeing the love bite on their mate later sets off another session of lovemaking.

- Alternate gently sucking with licking and nibbling. You may find this particularly effective on the inner thighs.
- Very gently suck and bite your lover's lower lip.
- Use blowing and breathing on your partner's body along with biting, too. (Breathing warm air on a delicate part of the body can be very pleasant for your partner.)

A gentle but firm bite at the moment of orgasm often heightens and punctuates the sensation, too. If it's too light it will go unnoticed . . . but if it's too harsh it will detract from genital sensation of the orgasm. Bite your partner while he or she is having an orgasm, but be very careful about having any part of your lover's body in your mouth when *you* orgasm; your jaw can spasm and clamp shut, causing severe injury.

Sexual Position #29

In this position the woman lies on her back on a bed, with her feet on the floor. She spreads her knees apart, and the man kneels in front of her and inserts his penis. He can hold her hips or legs to help himself thrust into her. He can also use one hand to stimulate her clitoris (it won't get much stimulation in this position otherwise).

This is a nice position for long, slow thrusts, combined with caressing her legs, hips, and breasts. The man can take a break now and again to lean forward and kiss her breasts and nipples, too.

Module 32

Breast Play

A woman's breasts are a sexual organ. One sometimes hears that the breasts are there to feed a baby, but that's not entirely true; certainly they have that function during a short period of a woman's life, but why does a woman have breasts when she *isn't* feeding a baby? Does that sound like a strange question? Consider, then, that the human is the only primate in which the female of the species has these large protuberances on her chest at *all* times, even when not feeding. In other primates the breasts all but disappear when there's no baby to feed.

Some biologists claim that a woman's breasts are clearly intended for the sexual excitement of the male of the species. And clearly they *do* excite the male—our society's fascination with the breast is testament to that fact. But they also excite the female—they are a highly erogenous zone. Or, at least, they excite some females; in fact some women can orgasm from breast and nipple stimulation alone. Paradoxically, though, the one technique in every man's sexual repertoire—sucking his partner's nipples and caressing her breasts—*doesn't* do anything for a significant number of women, perhaps as many as half.

Just how much breast play a woman enjoys varies enormously. Some can't get enough, and will lie back and take it all night if they can—and come several times, too. (Masters and Johnson found that about one woman in a hundred can have an orgasm from breast and nipple stimulation.) Others really don't get much out of it at all, and only put up with it because their partner enjoys it. Some studies, in fact, suggest that only one woman in two enjoys having her breasts caressed . . . though nine men out of ten enjoy doing it. (Or, are they doing it because they *think* the woman will enjoy it?) Also remember that for many women having the breasts touched and their nipples rubbed or sucked is quite uncomfortable during or right before menstruation.

Communication is important here. Talk about exactly what (and how much) feels good. A woman who enjoys breast stimulation will appreciate her man caressing her breasts before rushing down between her legs. A woman who gets nothing out of it will prefer that her man direct his attention elsewhere.

✤ ✤ The Man Has Breasts, Too ✤ ✤

But how about the man's chest and nipples? Have you ever considered the erotic potential of that area of a man's body? For most people the answer to that question is no. Most men go through their entire lives without ever considering that they could derive pleasure from their breasts (okay, their chests; the very word *breast* sounds strange in the context of a man, though it's quite correct), and while women sometimes caress their man's chest in passing, few direct active attention to that area.

Why *wouldn't* men's nipples be sensitive? They have the same network of nerves as a woman's. About fifty percent of men experience nipple erection during orgasm, and many have spontaneous nipple erection when sexually excited. Others are capable of nipple erection when their chest and nipples are gently caressed, kissed, and softly sucked. Of course the point is not simply to make his nipples stick up! Most men can enjoy this sort of stimulation of their chest and nipples, along with more aggressive squeezing and even pinching.

Why not experiment with breast play, providing pleasure to both partners by caressing, nibbling, and sucking? You can begin in a traditional manner, by caressing the woman's breasts. Most men are quite experienced at playing with a woman's breasts—after kissing, it's the first form of sexual contact they experienced, and they've enjoyed it ever since! Here are a few techniques you can use for extended breast play:

- The woman should tell the man what to do. He can begin by caressing, massaging, licking, or kissing her breasts, and she can then direct him in the activity she most enjoys. She should tell him exactly what to do and how. This little game of "show and tell" will teach him expert breast techniques that he can use later.
- Try swirling your fingers around the fullness of her breasts, and

gradually decrease the circumference of the swirls, moving inward toward the nipple with your fingers.

- Try the same thing with your mouth, kissing and licking in ever decreasing circles around her breasts, with the nipples as a final destination.
- Once the nipple is erect, slowly and gently breathe warm air onto it. Then try again, but tease the nipple with your tongue.
- Gently suck the nipple and surrounding breast into your mouth. Very gently pull your head away from the breast, while maintaining the suction—don't tug hard on the breast, you are just pulling gently. As you move away, slowly allow the breast and nipple to slip from your mouth.
- Suck firmly and noisily (if she likes noisy sucking).
- Using your open hand, grasp the full circumference of the breast, then slowly and gently lift your hand so that the fingers and fingernails very gently caress the breast, the aureola (the pinkish tissue around the nipple), and finally tug at the nipple itself.
- Softly knead the breasts with both hands. She should let him know how much pressure is pleasurable.
- Firmly rub the flat of your hands over the breasts and nipples.
- If the woman has very large breasts, try jiggling them a little. That provides a very pleasing feeling in the man's hands, and the woman may get a kick out of it too. Of course this works better if the woman is sitting up or standing.
- Wet your fingers with saliva, then very carefully and gently caress and roll the nipple between them. If she likes this, she might want more pressure. Some women enjoy a firm pinch, but others may find this painful.
- Place something tasty—a little wine, champagne, liqueur, chocolate, strawberry jam, whatever you like, really—onto the nipple, then suck it off, savoring the taste. You might moisten her nipples with her own vaginal juices—this can add an erotic flavor of sex.

✤ ✤ *I Want a Pearl Necklace!* ✤ ✤

For a nice variation, try a little intercourse involving penis and mammaries. If she has large breasts, the man can kneel above her, with the tip of his penis facing her neck, while she squeezes her breasts together around his penis. (Use some massage oil or some other kind of lubrication to make it feel even better.) With smaller breasts it may be easier for her to kneel between his open legs, lean down on his penis, and hold his penis to her chest while he squeezes her breasts together.

(Oh, what's a pearl necklace? You haven't figured it out? It's the gift the man gives to the woman in this position when he finally comes. You might want to rub it into the breasts when you've finished.)

✳ ✳ His Turn ✳ ✳

Don't let him feel left out. You can try many of the breast stimulation techniques on the man, too. The woman may also try rubbing her breasts and nipples over his, giving him a delicious flesh-on-flesh sensation. Try firm squeezes of the chest, and rubbing your hands all over his chest in a massaging motion. Pinching and sucking the nipples can be very exciting for him, too. The woman can kiss and caress a man's chest and nipples in the same way that she enjoys having him stimulate her breasts—she'll find that what works on her will probably work on him, and in turn he will see what she enjoys, and can employ the same techniques later.

By the way, it's sometimes said that there's a direct line from a woman's nipples to her clitoris. Suck the nipples, and she'll probably experience a twinge of pleasure between her legs, too. The same is often true for a man. Suck his nipples, and you may find that his penis hardens.

✳ ✳ Mini-69 ✳ ✳

If you find that the man does enjoy nipple stimulation, why not try a mini-sixty-nine. That's when you lie in a *soixante-neuf* position, but with your mouths at each other's breasts instead of each other's genitals. You could do this with both lying on your sides, or one on top of the other. It's probably easier to have the woman on top, as her breasts can drop into the man's mouth while she leans forward to reach his nipples with her mouth. (With him on top she might get a crick in the neck trying to reach his nipples.) You might use this as a prelude to oral sex. One of you lies on your back, and the other, beginning at the head, works his or her way down the body, spending a while sucking the nipples, then kissing and licking the belly and moving on until reaching the crotch.

Sexual Position #30

A woman who really enjoys breast stimulation will *love* it during intercourse. If you can manage to get all three going—vagina, clitoris, and nipples—you've really got it made. This position allows the man to suckle the nipples during intercourse. He has to bring his legs up, forcing her forward. Placing a large pillow under his head will help to bring his mouth closer to her breasts. And he may be able to place one hand down between her legs and caress her clitoris.

Module 33

Female Aggression

Here's a paradox for you. Many women feel that they should take a passive role, that it's up to their partner to take the active, aggressive role in sex. Many even feel that it would be somehow wrong to take an aggressive role, that a partner would feel that control had been taken away from him or wonder where she had learned such behavior. But men's attitudes don't reflect this. One of the most common complaints that men have about their lovers' sexual behavior is that they are not aggressive enough!

Strange, women feel that they should be passive—for fear of offending the man in many cases—while men often wish that the woman would take some action! In this module we're going to talk about how women can learn to be more active in sexual relations.

It's Okay!

Perhaps the first thing for a woman to understand is that it's okay to be forceful in sex, that she has the right to say what she wants (and what she doesn't want), and to initiate sexual activity. A lot has changed in attitudes about gender in the past quarter of a century. Women have become more confident, more strident in their demand for equal treatment . . . but in bed, it's often the same as ever. Men often feel that they make love to women, while women are made love to by men. It's almost a one-way thing, men giving and women receiving.

Talk about this. In most cases the woman will find that the man would be overjoyed to have a more aggressive partner. Why should the man have primary responsibility for sex? Why should he always be the one to initiate sexual activity? Why not take equal responsibility. Let him be the dominant partner when he wants to, let her be the dominant partner when *she* feels like it?

✻ ✻ Take Turns ✻ ✻

A good way to get started on a little sexual assertiveness training is to agree to take turns being "dominant." One evening the man takes the traditional male role, initiating sex and pretty much telling the woman the way it will proceed. On another night the woman takes over; it's her turn to begin sex, to tell her man what she wants him to do, to do to him things that will arouse him. All too often men feel that they do most of the work, that the woman spends most of her time lying back and waiting for the man to stimulate her in some way. Well, turnabout is fair play, and it's time for the woman to do the work, to try to please her man . . . and to take pleasure from him in any way she can.

A woman may need a little help with this. A particularly passive woman may not even know where to start. So discuss the process with your partner. The man suggests things that he enjoys, little tips and tricks that she can use to get him turned on. "Why don't we shower and you wash me?" "I like it when you spread my legs wide and bite my thighs," "I love it when you just push me down on the bed and get on top." Here's a little scenario the woman might use as a "starter."

1. Undress your man and give him a warm bath or shower. You are responsible for washing him, remember. He's allowed to just enjoy it and let you take the primary role . . . though there's nothing to stop him from touching and kissing you if he wants.
2. Dry him off and take him to bed. Give him a body massage with oil.
3. Roll him over on his back; lie next to him and kiss for a while, gently squeezing and caressing his testicles and penis, caressing his inner thighs.
4. Continue with foreplay, but you take the active role. Don't expect him to make any moves . . . caress his chest, kiss him on the neck and nibble his ears. Do all the things that you like him to do when he's making love to you.
5. Now kneel between his legs, or perhaps beside his torso, and take his penis in your mouth. Give him the very best oral sex you can imagine; do it with the sort of gusto and enthusiasm you appreciate from him when he performs cunnilingus.

6. If he wants intercourse straddle him and lower yourself onto his penis.
7. Do the things that you think will bring him pleasure—squeeze his penis with your vaginal muscles. Slide up and down on his penis with long, slow motions, so that the penis glides the full length in and out of you. "Churn" around, moving your hips in a circular motion so his penis moves around inside you in a circular motion. Imagine that you are a concubine in a harem and it's your job to bring as much pleasure to your master as possible, using your vagina as a wonderful sex toy. It won't take him long to come.
8. Stay on top of him for a while; you can lie down on him and kiss and hug. If you are lucky and he doesn't lose his erection, or regains one soon, you can use it to bring yourself pleasure. In the on-top position you may be able to direct the penis to your G spot, and can use your vaginal muscles to squeeze on his penis. (If he needs help with his next erection you might have to get off him and use your mouth or hands to get him back into action. Then remount and go on your way.)
9. Finish off by bringing a warm, soapy wash cloth and towel to clean him up.

You've probably heard the old saying that a man wants a lady in the drawing room and a whore in the bedroom. There's something to be learned from that. He may think of you as the most wonderful, sophisticated, ladylike woman in the world, but when he's interested in carnal pleasures all that goes out the window. He probably wants you to become a sexual animal. Use dirty language—tell him you enjoy his cock inside you, that you love to be fucked by him. Touch him anywhere and everywhere that appeals to you. Tell him what you want him to do to you, and don't be reticent about doing to him things you know he'll enjoy.

Of course, as with everything else sexual, there are no hard and fast rules. There are still men around who want to marry a virgin, who believe that normal women don't really enjoy sex, and who get jealous or angry if their partner shows too much sexual excitement or aggression. But that sort of man probably isn't reading this book.

Sexual Position #31

Make him lie back and take it; you're in control. He lies on his back, with his head and shoulders on a pillow, with his knees drawn up toward his chest. You sit astride him, gently pull his penis so that it points up, and lower yourself onto it. You'll both have to be fairly supple to try this position, and you may not use it for long, but try it, you'll probably find it fun. The man's in a sort of submissive, controlled position, while the woman rides high, controlling all the action.

Module 34

Regular Turn-Ons

Do you remember what it was like when you first met your partner? How easy was it to get turned on? If you are typical of most couples, all you had to do was walk into the same room as your partner to become instantly horny. Couples often report that when they first met they had sex almost continuously, that they would have sex almost every day—and if they didn't have sex, there had to be a very good reason. Sex several times a day is common for couples who have recently met; a quickie when they wake up, before getting ready for work; sex when they both get back from work; sex on the sofa while watching TV; and sex when they go to bed. Spontaneous sex is common too; walk into the bedroom while your partner is getting dressed to go out, and you'll probably end up missing the appointment. When you look back on the early days of a relationship it's sometimes hard to remember how you managed to earn money or feed yourselves.

You may never get back to those frenetic days, but it *is* possible to change your relationship, to find ways to turn each other on again. Instead of having sex just because "you need it," or because it's Saturday night, you can rekindle the fire in your belly. If you and your partner agree to carry out a program of everyday turn-ons, you'll find that sex will become exciting again.

The Daily Program

Here's a daily program you can use; it's virtually guaranteed to raise your turn-on level.

1. Each day, make sure you have at least ten mouth-to-mouth lingering kisses. Keep track, and if you find that you are below the target, make a point of getting enough kisses in to reach it.
2. Spend ten minutes or more of loving hugs and touching.
3. At least five minutes of rubbing, caressing, or patting of erogenous zones.
4. At least three times a day say "I love you."
5. At least one telephone call a day saying, "I was just thinking about you . . . " or "I was just thinking about last night and how wonderful you are."
6. At least once a week leave a note that expresses your love. If you are so inclined, write a little poem.
7. Once or twice a week set aside an evening for a romantic dinner.
8. Once a month or so go out of town, just the two of you, for a weekend of rest, love, recreation, and sex. (See Module 20: The Sexual Vacation.)

❧ ❧ Attention Is a Turn-On ❧ ❧

Simply providing your partner with attention is a great turn-on. Couples tend to reach a point at which they take each other for granted, or at least act that way. One of the best turn-ons, though, is to recognize and acknowledge the emotional support, love, and caring that you get from your lover. Reciprocate and return, in full measure, the love of your partner, and you'll find that love, and displays of affection, will increase. An unloved partner becomes a busy, indifferent, and inattentive mate.

It's typically a woman's complaint that her partner doesn't show her his appreciation, that he doesn't tell her he loves her and values her. Both partners can work on this, but it's often the man who needs to make extra effort to let his mate know how important she is to him. Be attentive, and make her feel as though she is the only woman that you desire.

❧ ❧ Remember the Turn-Ons ❧ ❧

One way to get turned on is to remember past sexual "adventures." Remember how it used to be when you were first together, and try to replicate those occasions. Try to do the things you used to do in the early days of your relationships:

- Have sex in different parts of the house, at different times of the day. Going out of your way to make sex a little different will add a spark to your sex. Whereas you could have sex and then go to sleep and forget about it, making it a little special in this way will make you wake up with a smile on your face. You'll find yourself thinking about it later the next day, too . . . which will get you horny all over again.

- At weekends or on vacations, after you've had breakfast take your lover by the hand and take him or her back to bed. You'll be rested and energetic, and sex will have an extra zip to it.

- Return to your "courting" activities. Go dancing. Go for walks in the park . . . and hold hands. When you eat at a restaurant, pick somewhere romantic and sit together so you can touch each other's hands (and legs, maybe). The man should bring his lover flowers, perhaps a single rose. This sort of activity makes women feel contented and desired, and brings out the gentle side of men.

- When you get home from work, hold each other and talk with each other. Confide that you had sexy thoughts about the other. (If you are following the modules in this book you almost certainly *will* have sexy thoughts!)

- When you are in bed together, talk about how you fantasized about this for hours: "On the way home from work I thought about you with every turn of the wheel." "At work I had trouble keeping my mind off your body." "I kept thinking of your lips and how I wanted to kiss them."

- Frequently hold, caress, and kiss each other. Don't wait until you are in the bedroom to kiss; make it a rule to kiss in at least three different rooms in the house. Occasionally stop what you are doing for long, sensual kisses.

- When you touch your partner and say that he or she is sexy, the sexual center within the brain will start the turn-on process in both of you. So hold your lover close with your hands on his or her buttocks and your pubic areas clinging together. Say something intimate or fun: "I love your tight little butt." Or "I like the way your breasts bounce. It turns me on." "I want to kiss you between your legs." Or "Let's have a party in your pants!"

- Rehearse being turned-on in your mind. Take time to fantasize about all the things you'd like to do with your partner—remember things you've done in the past that you found particularly exciting. Call your partner at work and explain what you plan to do to him or her when you get home. There's nothing more erotic than extended anticipation! (Make sure you follow through on your promises, though. It's not uncommon for one partner to promise some sensual activity, but not follow through at the end of the day because he or she simply feels too tired. After a while your partner will begin to assume your sexual promises won't be fulfilled—so your promises will no longer work as a turn-on.)

Sexual Position #32

Remember when you were both so hot for each other that you couldn't bother finding a bed for sex? Wherever you were, that was okay. Your home has plenty of furniture, all of it capable of being used as a sex prop. Take the following position, for instance. A simple chair is all that's required (though a little padding is nice). He sits on the chair, she moves forward and sits down onto his lap, his penis inside her. He can hold her close to him, and she can hold onto the back of the chair or his neck to steady herself. A nice position for long, lingering kisses.

Module 35

Slave for a Day

$\mathcal{H}$ ere's a nice little game in which one of you can absolve yourself of sexual responsibility, while the other can take full control. That is, you forget about your sexual desires, and give full responsibility for the "script" of your sexual encounter to your partner. One of you will become the slave, the other the master (actually, in this module, the mistress, as the woman's going to take the dominant role first). The slave agrees to follow the commands of the mistress, doing whatever the mistress demands (within reason: you should both agree that the slave can refuse an activity if it's dangerous or completely distasteful). There are a number of advantages to this game:

- If your partner is normally reticent about saying what she wants, being made to take control forces her to describe exactly what she likes you to do.
- Sometimes we fantasize about doing things that we are embarrassed to admit we would like to do. For instance, a man may fantasize about having sex with his partner and then eating her until she's clean. He may feel embarrassed to admit this, but if he's ordered to do so by his mistress he can comply without taking responsibility for the act. (The only problem is, of course, how he can communicate his desires to his partner without admitting to them!)

- Sex is less likely to be rushed. Instead of coming together and moving quickly to intercourse, the master or mistress is likely to demand certain services—such as massage or oral sex, for instance—perhaps over several hours, before getting to intercourse.
- The game gives the master or mistress the opportunity to think only of his or her own pleasure, something couples don't often get the chance to do.
- The master or mistress is likely to demand certain sexual acts that he or she wouldn't normally ask for. This game is a great way to learn about your partner's true desires.

❧ ❧ Ground Rules ❧ ❧

Here, then, are the ground rules for this game:

1. The object of the game is to provide pleasure to the master or mistress. Any pleasure derived by the slave is purely incidental, or whatever pleasure the master or mistress agrees to give the slave as a gift.
2. The slave agrees to comply with any reasonable (or very slightly unreasonable) demand. The slave should make an effort to comply with demands for sexual acts that he or she may find a bit distasteful.
3. There's a limit, though; the slave has the right to refuse acts that may be harmful or that the slave finds truly repugnant.
4. Agree on a time duration: the "next three hours," "from when we wake in the morning until midnight," and so on.

❧ ❧ On Your Marks ❧ ❧

Let's get started. We'll begin in this module by giving the woman control (the man gets his turn in the next module). Before you begin, think about the sorts of pleasures that you can demand from your man. Assuming you have allowed enough time, don't rush things. The ideal is to allow a complete day; then you can really take it easy, and indulge in sexual pleasures when the desire takes you. Consider pleasures that your partner may consider nonsexual; let him pamper you in some way. Here are a few examples to get you started (surely you'll quickly think of more!):

- Command your slave to fill a bubble bath, then to undress you and help you into the bath. While you are bathing he should wait attentively for your next command; to bring you a drink, to scrub your back, and so on. When you have finished your bath he should help you out and dry you off.

- Command your slave to prepare a massage area; place several large towels on the bed, for instance, or a thick blanket covered with towels in front of the fire in the living room. Then make him rub massage oil all over your body. Make him give you a complete massage (see Modules 12 and 13), and finish off by masturbating you or stimulating your G spot.
- Order your slave to disrobe and stay naked during his period of service, or perhaps wear a particular piece of clothing you like.
- If you trust him to do a good job, have your slave give you a pedicure or do your nails.
- How about demanding that your slave perform some kind of housework for you? (Naked, if you wish.) (Which reminds me of something Maureen Murphy once said: "The fantasy of every Australian man is to have two women—one cleaning and the other dusting.")
- Feel free to tease your slave. For instance, you might have him stand next to the sofa you are lying on, while you suck his penis. Then send him across the room before he comes. Be sure to keep him in sight so he can't relieve himself through masturbation.
- If you've teased him to the point of distraction, make him beg for sex—but require some sexual service before you provide him with any relief.
- If you decide to allow your slave some relief, you might limit him to masturbation. You can watch and touch yourself at the same time, with finger or vibrator. To make things particularly difficult for him, you can tell him that he mustn't come until you come.
- Command your slave to perform oral sex on you or to use a vibrator on you whenever it pleases you.
- If you are ready for sexual intercourse, feel free to indulge. There's no reason to avoid intercourse just because it will bring him relief. Still, make sure that you are in control. Tell him exactly what you want him to do, and what position you want to use. Make sure he understands that he's not to come until you give him permission.
- After intercourse your slave can clean you.
- Don't forget that slave-driving is hard work; your slave should prepare a banquet for you and hand-feed you. When you have finished you might allow him a little food, too—perhaps he could eat dessert off your body.

One more thing; don't be too cruel. Remember, it will soon be his turn!

Sexual Position #33

Sexual intercourse doesn't have to lead directly to orgasm. Sometimes it's nice to take your time and use a variety of positions that simply feel "nice." For a few minutes. This one, for instance, is a nice playing-around position. She's on top of him, with his penis inside her, and her legs toward his head. He holds her legs, she his. You can then rock together, and enjoy the unusual sensations. You probably won't use this for a long time—your arms are likely to tire—but it's very pleasant for a few minutes.

Slave for a Day

Module 36

Concubine for a Day

*N*ow the man's turn. If you've read the previous module, the woman has already had a chance to order her man around for a day (or a few hours, at least). Now it's the man's turn. Before you begin, make sure you read the previous module, in particular the "ground rules." The rules are the same for the man's enslavement of the woman. Here are a few things you might like to consider:

- Oral sex will be right at the top of many men's lists. The idea of being able to command that your partner suck your penis any time you wish is one that a lot of men find very attractive.

- Order your slave to dress up for you. Maybe in high heels, stockings, covered only by a filmy silk shawl. Or perhaps you want her to walk around naked for you, or wear a G string or crotchless panties.

- You might tie your slave down to the bed—use ribbons or some other kind of soft material. You can then use her any way you want; begin by kissing and licking all over her body. Have intercourse and come without worrying about her orgasm (remember, it's the master's right to take pleasure without giving it).

- You could leave your slave tied up until you are ready to have your sexual needs satisfied.

- There's no reason you shouldn't enjoy a full-body massage, too. Command your slave to prepare a massage area and to then rub oil into your body. She can finish with a massage of your genitals. Tell her exactly what you want, so you can extend your orgasm as long as you want.

- If you have considered prostate stimulation, but haven't yet been able to try it, this may be a good time to try, especially right after the massage.
- Take a bath or shower with your slave, and make her soap you all over.
- Take it easy, let her pamper you. You might spend much of the day on the sofa in front of the fire . . . hey, you can even watch football! Your harem girl can give you oral sex, or even intercourse, during half time, then go prepare a good meal. And you can even tell her to bring you a beer, without guilt. Just don't overdo the alcohol. (That would defeat the object of the game!)
- The idea of just lying back and enjoying yourself is very pleasing. We've all seen depictions of Roman emperors lying on a day bed, being fed grapes by beautiful women. Your concubine, too, can feed you grapes, as well as her nipples and vagina. Just lie back and let her bring whatever you need.

❧ ❧ A Quick Word About Bondage ❧ ❧

This game is not specifically about bondage; it's about ordering your partner to give you pleasure, not (necessarily) about S & M. In fact, if you are a couple that is already heavily into bondage, or sado-masochistic sex play, then you've probably already played slave games.

Still, you may find a little bondage exciting. You might wish to tie your partner down while you kiss and nibble all over his or her body. Or, even though you are in command, you might order your harem girl to do the same to you. Just because you are the master doesn't mean you can't order your concubine to act in what, at first sight, seems to be a dominant role.

If you do indulge in bondage, understand that there's a difference between play and the real thing! If you tie your partner up you should do so in such a manner that he or she can escape if need be. Many couples also use a special word, a code word that when uttered by the partner being "disciplined" means *Stop!* And understand that some people feel very uncomfortable with such games, regardless of the level of trust in the relationship (and it will require a lot of trust for any couple to play these games). If your partner really doesn't want to play, then forget it!

Sexual Position #34

She's yours for the day, use her however you wish. We suspect a lot of men will indulge in a variety of woman-on-top positions during their day of dominance. She does all the work, while he just lies back and enjoys it. He can caress her back and buttocks, fondle her breasts, and even stretch a little and run his hands between the cheeks of her buttocks and rub her vaginal lips. From this position she can move into a variety of other positions; sitting upright and squeezing on his penis with her PC muscles, leaning back with her hands on his legs for support, and so on.

Module 37

Copycat Lovers

*I*f you can just learn what pleases your lover, and if your lover can learn exactly what pleases you, you'll find your sex life immeasurably improved. Sad to say, many couples never really learn what each other truly likes. Early in their relationship they simply rush to sex, and have sex often. Pretty much everything seems to feel good, and the more often you have sex the more often you are likely to end up doing things that feel good, if only by accident. Then, as the relationship progresses, and as sex becomes less frequent, couples find themselves getting stuck in a rut.

Well, here's a way out of the rut. It's a game called "copycat," and it's a wonderful way for you to teach each other what you enjoy, by example. In the procedure I'm going to describe, the woman is doing the "teaching," but you should both take turns, perhaps on different nights.

1. Begin by using your hands on your man, any way you wish, except that you shouldn't touch his genitals. Imagine that you are your lover, and your lover is you. Do to him what you would enjoy him doing to you. For instance, caress his chest and nipples in the way that you would enjoy him caressing *your* breasts and nipples. Spend five minutes touching his body.

2. Now it's the man's turn. He should touch your body, copying exactly what you did, the way you caressed and touched him. He should spend the same amount of time.

3. Now you use your mouth on your lover. Place your mouth wherever you

wish—except his genitals—kissing, licking, sucking, and nibbling. Spend five minutes or so doing this.

4. Now the man should copy, as closely as possible, what you did to him, using his mouth on you.

5. Now you should use your hands on his genitals for five minutes or so. Just your hands, not your mouth yet. This is perhaps the most difficult part of the game, because there's no direct relationship between manually stimulating the man's genitals and yours. Still, you can use the same sort of caresses and strokes you enjoy. Don't worry about giving him a great "hand job," try to demonstrate the form of manual stimulation you enjoy—the same firmness or lightness of touch, for instance.

6. Now it's his turn to use his hands on your genitals, transferring the techniques you showed him the best he can.

7. You now use your mouth on his genitals. Don't do what you would normally do to provide him with pleasure, though. Use the sort of licks and sucks that you would enjoy on your vagina and clitoris. Of course it's difficult to make a direct comparison between the two sets of genitals, but you might think of the head of his penis as your clitoris, and consider the testicles and shaft of the penis as your vagina.

8. The man then takes over and tries to replicate your mouth actions, using his mouth on your vagina and clitoris.

9. Now you bring him to orgasm, any way you want. Don't worry about reaching an orgasm yourself. For instance, if you choose to use your vagina, just make him come without worrying if you come first.

10. Finally, he brings you to orgasm, using the same method. If you used your hand, he should use his hand; if you used your mouth, he should use his mouth; if you used your vagina, he should use his penis (he may need to wait a few minutes, though, to get another erection).

The idea of this game is to break up the mechanical routine of sex that so many couples fall into. It allows each person both to lie back and enjoy sex as well as to take a more active role, and provides an equal share of time for each activity. You'll learn what your partner enjoys, and you'll be able to lie back and delight in the pleasure of being the object of your partner's sexual caresses.

Use this game again sometime, swapping roles. You'll find that the sex play takes a slightly different "route" depending on which partner "leads off" in this game. In fact play a few times and you may find that it's different each time, depending on the mood of the lead partner.

Alex Comfort, author of *Joy of Sex*, wrote this: "Remember, your partner will do to you what they really want done to them—being aware of this is the great secret of communicating sex." So even when you are not playing the copy-cat game, think about what your partner is doing to you. There's a good chance that he or she would be very pleased if you reciprocated, by copying those actions. A partner who often performs oral sex on you probably greatly enjoys having you perform oral sex. A partner who likes to nibble and kiss your inner thighs quite likely enjoys having his or her inner thighs kissed and nibbled, too. Persons who enjoy sucking your nipples will probably derive great pleasure from having their nipples sucked, too. Pay attention to your partner's actions, and you'll learn a lot.

Sexual Position #35

This position affords quite deep penetration. He kneels in front of her and, with her legs wide apart, enters her. She then wraps her legs around his waist, and pulls herself toward him. Or she can also raise her legs and put them over his shoulders. In fact you might want to try that position after a few minutes of the legs-around-the-waist position, because it provides *very* deep penetration.

References

Castleman, Michael. *Sexual Solutions: A Guide for Men and Women Who Love Them.* Simon and Schuster, 1989.

Comfort, Alex. *Joy of Sex.* Crown Books, 1972.

Comfort, Alex. *More Joy: A Lovemaking Companion to The Joy of Sex [More Joy of Sex].* Crown Books, 1974.

Gebhard, Paul H., Alan B. Johnson. *The Kinsey* Data. The W.B. Saunders Company. 1979.

Hite, Shere. *The Hite Report on Male Sexuality.* Alfred A. Knopf, 1981.

Kolodny, Robert C., Virginia E. Johnson, William H. Masters. *Textbook of Sexual Medicine.* Little, Brown, 1979.

Krane, Robert J., Mike B. Siroky, Erwin Goldstein. *Male Sexual Dysfunction.* Little, Brown, 1983.

Masters, William H., Virginia E. Johnson. *Human Sexual Inadequacy.* Little, Brown, 1970.

Masters, William H., Virginia E. Johnson, Robert C. Kolodny. *Human Sexuality.* Little, Brown, 1985.

Masters, William H., Virginia E. Johnson, Robert C. Kolodny. *Masters and Johnson on Sex and Human Loving.* Little, Brown, 1986.

Zilberbeld, Bernie. *Male Sexuality.* Bantam Books, 1978.